THE HAPPINESS OF DOGS

Also by Mark Rowlands

A Good Life: Philosophy from Cradle to Grave

Running with the Pack: Thoughts From the Road on Meaning and Mortality

The Philosopher and the Wolf: Lessons From the Wild on Love, Death and Happiness

The Happiness of Dogs

Why the Unexamined Life
Is Most Worth Living

Mark Rowlands

GRANTA

Granta Publications, 12 Addison Avenue, London W11 4QR

First published in Great Britain by Granta Books, 2024

Copyright © Mark Rowlands, 2024

Mark Rowlands has asserted his moral right under the Copyright, Designs and Patents Act, 1988, to be identified as the author of this work.

All rights reserved.
This book is copyright material and must not be copied, reproduced, transferred, distributed, leased, licensed or publicly performed or used in any way except as specifically permitted in writing by the publisher, as allowed under the terms and conditions under which it was purchased or as strictly permitted by applicable copyright law. Any unauthorized distribution or use of this text may be a direct infringement of the author's and publisher's rights, and those responsible may be liable in law accordingly.

A CIP catalogue record for this book is available from the British Library.

1 3 5 7 9 10 8 6 4 2

ISBN 978 1 80351 032 3 (hardback)
ISBN 978 1 80351 245 7 (trade paperback)
ISBN 978 1 80351 034 7 (ebook)

Typeset in Melior by M Rules

Printed and bound by CPI Group (UK) Ltd, Croydon, CR0 4YY
www.granta.com

For Emma

Up they rose
As from unrest, and, each the other viewing,
Soon found their eyes how opened, and their minds
How darkened. Innocence, that as a veil
Had shadowed them from knowing ill, was gone;
Just confidence, and native righteousness,
And honour, from about them, naked left
To guilty Shame.

—John Milton, *Paradise Lost*

Contents

	Preface	1
1	Shadow's Rock	7
2	The Unexamined Life	30
3	Mirror, Mirror	53
4	A Gambler's Freedom	86
5	Good Dogs	110
6	A Design for Life	147
7	Just Dogs with the Yips	171
8	Sometimes Toward Eden	197
9	Further Reading	231
	Acknowledgements	241
	Index	242

Preface

I think the ancient Greek philosopher Socrates was correct when he claimed that dogs are natural philosophers. But if a dog could write a book of philosophy, what would it look like?

The more time I spend with dogs – and, a few dogless years in my twenties aside, I have spent all my life with them – the more I am convinced they can teach us a thing or two about life, what is important in it, and how to live it. Philosophers think hard about these questions and do their best to answer them, with limited success. But dogs answer them effortlessly and decisively. The difference is that the human philosophers think about these questions. Dogs, on the other hand, live them. It is through their lives that they impart philosophical lessons, even though they have no idea what philosophy is.

Here is a very recent lesson. In fact, it is being taught as I type these words. I have just asked Shadow a question: 'Do you want to come with?' Shadow is a German shepherd and my question has caused him to explode

The Happiness of Dogs

into one of his customary expressions of delight: jumping, spinning, then running to fetch his leash. He doesn't stop there. Tossing the leash in the air so that it will land on his back, he then endeavours to locate the noose – it is a slip leash – so he can insert his head through it. I wouldn't say it works every time – his chances of success depend on how the leash falls on his back – but his track record in self-leashing is already impressive and always improving.

From the intensity of the excitement exhibited, you would think I had just informed Shadow that we were going to visit a dog park crammed fence to fence with female German shepherds in the middle of their oestrus stage. But that's not going to happen and he knows it. He knows we are simply going to pick up my son from school. This is the time of day we do it, and like all dogs, he is keenly attuned to the day's rhythms. In fact, he has been staring at me for the last twenty minutes, willing me to say the magic words. He knows little of interest will occur on this journey, the mercurial nature of Miami drivers notwithstanding. He won't get out of the car and have a run. He is not going to meet any other dogs. We will drive, pull into the school, collect my son, and drive straight back to the house. Shadow is an intelligent dog and we've been doing this for a long time; he knows exactly how it will play out. Nevertheless, his reaction is always the same. Unparalleled excitement. Barely containable, frequently self-leashing, exuberance. If I exhibited this kind of excitement, you could be certain that I

Preface

was having the best minute of the best day of my life. Whenever this happens – and it happens every school day – I think to myself: *Why can't I feel like that?* Many humans will think dogs behave like that because they are stupid. But if that is what being stupid is, I wish someone would sign me up.

I see something else in Shadow's response: the ability to take pleasure in the smallest things that life has to offer. To love life so much that whenever anything good happens, no matter how marginally positive, one always thinks: *This – this! – is the best thing that has ever happened to me!* That doesn't seem stupid at all. Life, as we all know, can be cruel. Indeed, in the end, it almost always will be cruel. To find such happiness in the smallest things seems to be a magnificent triumph over cruelty and despair. A triumph, ultimately, over life. Why, I often wonder, can't I triumph over life too?

In all of this, there is a lesson. It is a lesson repeated every school day – dog pedagogy involves a lot of repetition – and it is difficult to think of this lesson as anything other than philosophical. It is a lesson about life's meaning. Albert Camus, the great existentialist philosopher, claimed that there is 'only one really serious philosophical problem, and that is suicide. Deciding whether or not life is worth living is to answer the fundamental question in philosophy.' All the other questions of philosophers, he claimed, are mere games. This question is a way of asking about the meaning of life. Camus's thought was that what makes life worth the trouble is, precisely, life's meaning, so if you can work out the former you have successfully understood the latter. Without even understanding that there was a question to be answered, Shadow has answered it, and has done so with a conviction which Camus and I are incapable of achieving. His answer is simple: *everything!* There is, I have to admit, a certain lack of nuance, like all canine answers to philosophical questions; subtlety is not a notable strength of dogs. Nevertheless, there is something fundamentally promising in this answer. If not exactly correct, it is in the vicinity of correct, and it points in the general direction of a correct answer. It is something, in other words, that provides excellent raw material for a clever, nuanced ape to usefully work with. Dogs are the ideas people; they are creative. I am a low-level simian drudge, only here to fill in the details.

The meaning of life is far from a dog's only excursion into matters philosophical. If you know how to look, you will find them weighing in on such questions as the nature of consciousness, what it means to be moral, freedom and its scope and limits, and the nature of rationality. They do this effortlessly, without understanding that they are weighing in on anything at all, let alone a philosophical dispute. Rather than think about the answers to these questions, they live them. And if there is one thing that animates all their answers – that binds these answers together into a unified whole – it is love. The love of life and action. Love is the cornerstone of any canine philosophy: love and its cognates, such as happiness and commitment.

Preface

In the authentic happiness Shadow finds in even the most banal of activities, he has a commitment to life and action that we humans find so hard to emulate. The reason is that something happened to us that made us decisively different from dogs – what we might think of as the great divergence. It is not, fundamentally, a biological divergence, although it would have been, at least partially, rooted in biology. It is a divergence in consciousness. Our consciousness is very different to that of dogs. We think this makes us better, but I find very little evidence for the truth of this assertion, and I suspect the opposite is true. This divergence has taken from us a certain kind of happiness; that is not to say that it makes such happiness impossible for us to attain, just much more difficult. For a dog, happiness comes effortlessly, but for us it is a hard-won, sometimes bitter achievement.

We humans think and we think, and we think some more; we are unnatural philosophers. We devise answers to our questions, and sometimes these satisfy us for a time and sometimes they do not. Dissatisfaction is always our eventual lot. The distinctive stench of doubt pervades our efforts, and it is no coincidence that when philosophy was born in ancient Athens, it was born in doubt. Socrates' philosophy was decisively shaped by the idea that he knew nothing. And when philosophy was reborn during the Enlightenment, it happened in a similar state of doubt, this time the methodological doubt of René Descartes. Philosophy has always been concerned with what we can know because, deep down, we suspect we don't know very much at all.

Dogs are natural philosophers. What we know, if we know anything, we know through thinking; dogs in comparison know through living. And in the unbridled happiness of dogs – in their love of life and their utter commitment to their actions which I see so joyously enacted in Shadow today – we can find answers to many of the traditional problems of philosophy. In the poem 'Fern Hill', his ode to childhood, Dylan Thomas wrote that though time held him green and dying, he sang in his chains like the sea. Time holds us all green and dying, dogs and humans alike. But, unlike us, dogs never forgot how to sing. That is what this book is about.

1

Shadow's Rock

One must imagine Sisyphus happy.

—Albert Camus, *The Myth of Sisyphus*

Each morning, Shadow and I exit the gate at the bottom of the garden and walk out on to the bank of the canal that lies behind our house. He is leashed for the first few seconds, while I make sure the coast is clear. We could do without any surprises – such as the unexpected appearance of the American bulldog who lives next door, for whom Shadow has an occasionally violent antipathy that is mutual. As I prepare to unleash him, he thrashes his head and shoulders back and forth, the excitement too much to contain. Then he is gone, a bullet from a gun. North. One hundred metres. Two. Three. Four. Before slowly coming to a halt, turning around, and trotting back to me. As he gets closer, his pace gradually increases, each stride longer and quicker than the one before. To me. And past me. South. One hundred metres. Two. Maybe three – it depends on how he is feeling. He rarely makes four on the second leg these days. Neither of us is as young as we used to be. Finally, he breaks his stride, turns wide, and swaggers back to me.

We are all immigrants here, on this canal in Miami. I am from the United Kingdom, but this is my sixteenth year of South Florida sunshine. Shadow has lived here for six of those years. He was born in the smallish town of Homburg, near Saarbrücken, on the westernmost edge of Germany. His ancestors, however, originated from further to the east, for he is an East German working-line shepherd. As is common for the East German dogs, he's big for a shepherd, pushing thirty inches at the withers, and weighing in just a little shy of 100 pounds. He appears to be completely jet black, but if you look closely, between his toes, you will see that the fur is light brown, making him, technically, a bicolour. For reasons I shall shortly outline, I wouldn't advise you to get close enough to look between his toes.

The other émigrés on this bank are the iguanas – green iguanas – that hail originally from South and Central America. They are the reason for Shadow's frenzied charge up and down the canal. Later, in the sweltering heat of the afternoon, they will form the sprawling *mess* that spawns their collective noun. But at this time of the morning, neither early nor late, they line the banks, spaced at semi-regular intervals. On Shadow's initial northerly sortie there may be thirty to forty iguanas lined up around 10 metres apart; the southern counterpart is less predictable since the iguanas will, by then, have a sense that something is up and will have taken the appropriate precautions. As Shadow's thundering footsteps draw unacceptably close, the iguanas successively peel off into the water, one after the other. In the 1930s, there was a synchronized-swimming ensemble devised and orchestrated by the Hollywood director Busby Berkeley. One of their routines involved them lining up at the edge of a swimming pool and then diving in, sideways, one after the other. The overall visual effect was like the opening of one of those old-fashioned folding hand fans. Collectively, the iguanas achieve something remarkably like this iconic early Hollywood display – just somewhat more, you know, *reptilian*.

The result of Shadow's determined efforts is that each morning, scores of iguanas are exiled to the other side of the canal. The afternoon walk will see Shadow bouncing along his side of the bank, scowling at the hundreds of iguanas that now lie on the other side in their characteristic afternoon mess as if to say, 'Oh yes, you better stay over there!' But while they might remember the wisdom of doing so during the day, the night is a time of forgetting for iguanas. Come the morning they will have returned to Shadow's bank of the canal, and this little piece of theatre will be repeated, down to the minutest of details.

This unfolding daily drama is recognizably Sisyphean. In Greek mythology, Sisyphus was a mortal who offended the gods and paid the price with an eternally repeated monotonous task. While he was alive, Sisyphus had generally been accepted to be a tricky and unpleasant customer. Death didn't seem to change him much. Having convinced the gods to let him return to earth on an urgent errand – largely one of admonishing his wife for her inadequate funerary provision – Sisyphus subsequently refused to return to the underworld. The punishment handed down by the gods was ingenious and severe. Sisyphus was condemned to roll an immense rock up a hill. Each time he reached the summit – after who knows how long of gruelling labour – the rock would slip from his grasp and roll back to the bottom of the hill. Having followed it down, he would have to start pushing it to the top all over again. And that, for Sisyphus, was that – for all eternity.

The afterlife of Sisyphus is usually understood as the perfect embodiment of a meaningless life. While standard versions of the myth emphasize the immensity of the rock and the backbreaking effort required of Sisyphus to advance it even a single step, this does not capture the real malice of the punishment. Imagine, for example, that the enormous rock is replaced by a smallish pebble, one that Sisyphus can easily carry in his hand or slip into his pocket. His task would now be less onerous, but I doubt that its nastiness would have significantly diminished. He must still return each time to the foot of the hill and begin his task again. The cruelty of his punishment stems not from its difficulty but from its pointlessness. No matter what Sisyphus does, he can never succeed – because there is nothing in this task that would count as success or failure. Whether he reaches the summit or not, the rock will always find its way back to the bottom of the hill, where he must begin his task all over again. Sisyphus rolls the rock to the summit only so that he can do so again. And again. And again ...

In its portrayal of meaninglessness as repetitive activity that aims only at the continuation of itself, the myth of Sisyphus is often taken as an allegory of human life. On any given day, any given human might wake up, fight their way through the daily commute, board the same train today as they did on countless days before, reach an office where, minor details aside, they do the same things today as they did yesterday, and will do tomorrow. The net result of all of this? Probably very little. Any achievements will soon be wiped away by time's remorseless tide. All through this person's work day, the outward commute, the homeward commute, the eight hours or more in between, they are surrounded by other people doing pretty much the same things, with the same results, or lack thereof. Perhaps these people are happy or perhaps they are not. They do it anyway. Waiting for them at home, perhaps, are partners and children – children who will one day grow up and do the same kinds of things as their parents, with the same kinds of results, their lives mere notational variants on those of their forebears. Each step Sisyphus takes up his hill is like a day in the life of such a person. We are all, in this sense, Sisyphus. The only difference is that Sisyphus returns to the foot of his hill while we leave that task to our children (if we have them).

The myth of Sisyphus, therefore, poses a serious challenge to the idea that human life can be meaningful. A Sisyphean life appears to be meaningless, and our lives appear to be Sisyphean. In the face of this challenge, we can deny that our lives are Sisyphean, or we can deny that a Sisyphean life is necessarily a meaningless one. Shadow, perhaps more than anyone, has convinced me of the power and prospects of the second option.

Each morning, Shadow exiles the iguanas to the far bank. The very next morning they will have returned, and Shadow must begin his efforts all over again. The iguanas are Shadow's rock. But not only does this seem to be one of the most enjoyable parts of Shadow's life, it is also, my intuition convinces me, one of the most meaningful parts of it. A Sisyphean life, defined by repetitive activity that aims only at its own repetition, cannot, we are told by pretty much everyone who has thought about this issue, be meaningful. But if Shadow is right, it can. The challenge of Sisyphus is here answered by the unstinting zeal of a dog. Finding meaning in life is hard for us, but easy for dogs. The consequences of this insight are profound and unsettling.

We may all be immigrants on the banks of this canal, but the iguanas are undocumented and, as such, are often treated harshly by the local authorities. They are classified as 'invasive' – meaning that they are a non-native species that is doing damage to the local ecosystem. This is an unpleasant and deeply ironic accusation if ever there was one, issuing as it does from the mouth of the first and by far the most accomplished invasive species. We came out of Africa and invaded everywhere; and now we facilitate other invasive species by letting them hitch a ride on our ships and aeroplanes. The iguanas are sporadically subjected to various extermination attempts, almost always involving poisoning. It's a sad and futile undertaking, Sisyphean in its way. Within a few weeks the numbers will have been replenished from surrounding neighbourhoods. But those weeks between local extinction and restoration are tough for both me and Shadow, though admittedly for different reasons.

For my part, I like our iguanas. I have named many of them. In the most recent generation, there is *Cocky* – he has a very high flight threshold, always the last and most reluctant to seek refuge in the canal. Then there is *Bolt* – he has a crossbow bolt sticking out of his back. It doesn't seem to slow him down too much. I once half-heartedly tried to catch him to get a closer look or perhaps even remove it, but couldn't get close. There is *Stripey* – largely self-explanatory, that one. Most impressively, there is *Big Poppy*. That dude is five feet long! Just for a moment, when I first saw him out of the corner of my eye, I thought he was a gator. It gave me quite a shock. After each poisoning, as the new immigrant influx rolls in, I, a dispirited Adam in his Garden of Eden, must begin anew my task of naming the animals.

Whatever sadness I feel, however, is nothing compared with the devastation suffered by Shadow. The first morning after the great poisoning is always, for him, one of confused desolation. His initial northerly charge begins with its usual drama and pomp, only to gradually peter out as he realizes nothing is running from him, and there are no panicked plunges into the water. He tries to change things up a little; a random charge here, a little sprint there, to see if it will disturb any hiders. To no avail. Eventually he looks me in the eye quizzically, as dogs do when they have encountered a problem they cannot solve. The rest of the morning walk is merely Shadow going through the motions – a pallid echo of his normal self. It is as if someone stole Sisyphus's rock in the middle of the night. But when he awoke, he did not rejoice, as we might not unreasonably have assumed he would, but instead retreated into despair. Taking away Shadow's rock has produced not joy but deep existential pain. It is as if, contrary to everything we thought, Sisyphus's rock turned out to be not his damnation but his happiness.

What is the difference between Shadow and Sisyphus such that essentially the same life – a life with the same overall shape and theme – could be positively overflowing with meaning when lived by one and utterly bereft of meaning when lived by the other? An obvious, perhaps facile, answer is that Shadow is happy whereas Sisyphus is not. But this is only a relatively small part of the story. After all, we can find ways of making Sisyphus happy without imbuing his existence with any sort of meaning. Imagine, for example, that the gods decided to bestow upon Sisyphus a modicum of mercy. The rock, the hill, the neverending, pointless labour all remained non-negotiable as far as the gods were concerned, but the mercy of the gods was to change Sisyphus's attitude to these things. Far from hating them, as we must assume he did in the standard version of the myth, Sisyphus — due to the gods' intervention — now loves these things intensely. He is never happier than when rolling large boulders up steep hills, and the gods have offered him the eternal fulfilment of this strange desire.

I think it is undeniable that Sisyphus would be much happier in this version of the myth. Some might think that this effectively transforms his punishment into a reward, or something more like a reward. But this does not mean his life is any more meaningful. On the contrary, it is arguable that his life is now even less so. In the standard version of the myth, it is possible to see in Sisyphus a certain kind of nobility. Powerful but vicious beings have imposed on Sisyphus his grim fate. There is nothing he can do to change this fate — not even die. He understands the hopelessness of his situation, the inevitability and inescapability of his predicament. However, in his contempt for the gods

The Happiness of Dogs

who have imposed this fate on him, and in his refusal to be broken by them or it, he endows his life with a kind of tragic, and savage, dignity. This is, perhaps, what the existentialist philosopher Albert Camus had in mind when he concluded his essay 'The Myth of Sisyphus' with the claim – or perhaps it was advice – that *one must imagine Sisyphus happy*. Whether or not this is what Camus intended, this savage dignity is lost in this re-imagining of a happy Sisyphus. The dignified Sisyphus has been replaced by a deluded Sisyphus, a noticeably dumber version of Sisyphus than the one who inhabits the traditional myth.

Re-imagining the myth in this way throws into sharp relief the contrast between the happiness of Shadow and that of the deluded Sisyphus, tricked by the gods. Sisyphus's happiness is not part of who or what he is; it comes not from him but from the gods. The happiness of Shadow, on the other hand, is a happiness that originates in, and erupts from, his deepest nature. It is difficult to exaggerate how important this point will turn out to be.

It is no accident that such a significant part of Shadow's life is tied to this canal bank adjoining our home. It is isolated, and we are not likely to encounter anyone here. And if we do, we'll see them coming a long way off. *Character is destiny*, as my favourite pre-Socratic philosopher, Heraclitus of Ephesus, once remarked.

Shadow's Rock

Shadow's character is dominated by one notable trait: *aggression*. To be honest, in a lifetime spent with dogs, I've never seen anything like it. I certainly hope it was nothing I did. I don't think it was – as far as I remember, he was always like that, for as long as I have known him. When he was a three-month-old puppy, having been living with us for only a couple of days, I took him into my office in the Philosophy Department at the University of Miami. His very first act there was to tear into my colleague's dog, James (named after the philosopher and psychologist William James), a sharpeagle (that is, a sharpei/beagle mix). I had to pull Shadow off, whereupon he bit me too. Three months old, and already with severe anger-management issues. The reasons for this presumably stem from his history which, like all personal histories, began long before he was born.

Shadow issues from a long line of *Schutzhunde*: protection dogs. The word 'Schutzhund' denotes both a type of training that a dog can undergo and a dog that has successfully completed this training. The training itself is a little like martial arts for dogs. It involves three elements: obedience, tracking and protection, and Schutzhund attainment comes in three levels – Schutzhund 1, 2 and 3, with 3 being the highest. I have Shadow's pedigree, tracing back to his great-great-grandparents. Of the thirty-two dogs listed, thirty-one were Schutzhund 3. The other one, the black sheep slacker of the family – yes, I'm talking about you, Haifa vom Schotterhof – was Schutzhund 2.

The Happiness of Dogs

It is doubtful that Shadow's Schutzhund lineage explains his aggression, certainly not on its own. If anything, the opposite may be true. Some protection-dog professionals – those who buy and train dogs for protection work – think that the Schutzhund programme might have even mitigated Shadow's aggression. Schutzhund, some tell me, has ruined the German shepherd as a serious protection prospect. The theory is that the obedience component of Schutzhund militates against the truly aggressive dog, since such a dog would never tolerate the obedience part of the training, or at least not every aspect of it. Since attainment of at least Schutzhund 1 is a condition of being allowed to breed papered German shepherds in Germany, these naysayers believe that, through the Schutzhund programme, aggression has slowly been weeded out of the gene pool. Instead, those same protection-dog professionals now tend to buy Dutch Shepherds – a semi-amorphous category that includes the Belgian Malinois as well as the more stereotypical wire-haired Dutch herding dog. I don't know if this assessment of the Schutzhund programme is correct. But, if it is, I'm pretty sure Shadow never got the memo.

More relevant might be his specifically East German line. Many think that East German working-line shepherds are better suited to police and military applications than to the family hearth. For example, the K9 University of Chicago (whatever that is) tells us that such dogs 'often work as police dogs, military dogs, and search and rescue dogs. This type of German Shepherd is very intelligent but can be aggressive towards strangers. They often make better working or guard dogs than pets.' This strikes me as spot on, and I gather that many of Shadow's extended family did, in fact, work in these fields. It may be that Shadow would have been better off doing so too. By the time this possibility dawned on me, it was too late. He was a deeply loved member of the family, and, paradoxical though this may seem for such an aggressive dog, he returned that love in spades.

Dog trainers distinguish between two forms of aggression: *active* and *reactive*. Active aggression, also known as *prey drive*, is responsible for Shadow's daily charges up and down the canal bank in pursuit of iguanas – and ducks, and, at various times of the year, egrets, ibises, vultures, and other sundry fauna. The vultures of winter are a particular favourite of his, especially when they cluster on the ground in *wake* formation. I have never seen Shadow happier than when charging into the middle of a wake of vultures – the bigger the better – and scattering them to the four winds. In those moments, he reminds me of Conan the Barbarian's famous answer to his master's philosophical question, *What is best in life?*, which seems to capture Shadow's attitude towards vultures quite nicely: something along the lines of crushing your enemies, driving them before you and hearing the lamentations of their women. Even a soaring aerial congress is often enough to set him off. He knows what they are. And whoever said dogs can't look up has never seen Shadow surveying the sky above him.

From the perspective of a dog trainer, there's nothing better than active aggression. This aggression gives the trainer the means of educating the dog by providing it with a powerful motivation to learn. With such a dog, food rewards will only take you so far. What a dog like this really wants is something to chase – a ball, a frisbee, anything that moves in a way that mimics, even loosely, prey. That's how I trained Shadow in obedience: the standard Schutzhund M.O. is begin with food, and then work up to inanimate chaseable things. The animate chaseable things that line the canal bank are the final stage in his education. After the initial surges have tempered him a little, we sometimes use the iguanas in other aspects of his training too. A heel, a sit, a down, or even a long down in the vicinity of a bemused iguana, taut, tense, and primed to plunge into the waiting canal, is always useful to keep Shadow up to date concerning the demands of obedience. And the eventual release – a joyful ode to puissance – is something to behold.

While active aggression is excellent for the purposes of obedience training, its counterpart – *reactive aggression* – is far less useful. The notion of *trespass* unites many of the multifarious forms of reactive aggression: someone has come too close to the triggering stimulus – food (or another resource such as a toy), family or territory. Shadow's reactivity seems to be fundamentally territorial, but territory, for him, is a movable feast. His territory is wherever he is. He won't go out of his way to encroach on *your* territory, but if you encroach on his without permission – and if you are not a member of the family you never have permission – he will attack, offering no concessions and sometimes little overt warning.

We have turned this proclivity of his into games. He always appreciates it when I arrange for someone to show up in a bite suit, although that is reserved for special occasions such as birthdays. But Shadow's favourite day-to-day game when he was still a young dog – six to eighteen months of age – was one he played with certain, bolder, members of the student body at the University of Miami, where I teach. I used to take him to classes with me in those days. He would lie at the front of the class as I lectured, glaring balefully at the students. No one challenged their grades in my classes, I assure you. Since then – and the day this was implemented was a very sad day for Shadow – dogs have been banned from the university's indoor spaces. Ironically, this had nothing to do with Shadow. Allergies were the reason they gave. I think I'm allergic to every tree, shrub, flower and blade of grass on that noticeably arboreal campus – my sinuses certainly contend that this is so – but no one is talking about cutting all these down for me. Banning Shadow on account of allergies is a little like locking up Al Capone for tax evasion. It works, but it misses the point. If the

The Happiness of Dogs

university had wanted a more urgent and respectable reason for the new rule, all they had to do was visit my PHI 381 Existentialism class, Tuesdays and Thursdays, at around 3.15 p.m.

When the class was over, some of the more daring students used to help me with Shadow's training. I'd have him on a leash (obviously), and a student, standing just out of range, would take a hard step towards Shadow, their front foot slapping dramatically on the floor. Shadow would launch himself directly at the student, his teeth coming up short – clanking on empty air in the general vicinity of the student's throat – as the leash did its crucial work. Then I would quickly step in with a *Platz!* – Down! – command, whereupon he would, believe it or not, dutifully lie down. I would congratulate him. We would do it all over again until he got tired, or until the students had to go to their next classes. To be honest, I think Shadow found the Platz command quite a relief. Perhaps his biological history had made him feel he *should* attack, but I think he quite liked these students – if it is possible to like someone distrustfully – and didn't really want to bite them. He certainly seemed to look forward to this impromptu training. He knew exactly what was going to happen after class, and you could see his excitement building the longer the class went on.

This classroom activity is an example of what is known as *proofing* – in this case, *proofing the down*. You've taught the dog to down. Great. Now you must proof it: make sure the dog will down or maintain the down whenever required. My lectures were an hour and fifteen minutes of maintaining the long down – in the face of duress or distractions. A student comes into class late – an infraction punishable by dismemberment as far as Shadow is concerned – but too bad: he still has to stay in the down position. The after-class exercises with the students were to teach him to down-in-motion when his blood is up. When I relate this story, the reaction I often get is: why were you teaching him to be vicious? I was not, in fact, teaching him to be anything at all, merely drawing on what he already was with a view to controlling, and ideally mitigating, it. He was already reactively aggressive, and what I was trying to do was proof against its most damaging expressions.

We continue this work every day on the canal bank. Once Shadow has the northerly and southerly charges out of his system, we get to work with sits and downs, long downs, downs in motion (definitely a work-on) and recalls. Proofing is naturally provided by the local fauna. Ducks are sometimes quite useful. I don't want Shadow killing ducks. I don't want him killing iguanas, either, but I don't worry about them: they are too fast, and he never catches them. Most of the time, I don't have to worry about ducks either, because they will be standing on the edge of the bank, ready to spring into the air when Shadow charges towards them. Occasionally, however, a family of Muscovy ducks might appear from the bushes, with Shadow situated between them and the sanctuary of the canal.

The Happiness of Dogs

He would be on top of them before they begin their rather clumsy, protracted take-offs. At such times, 'Platz!' suddenly becomes the most important word in the universe of those ducks. Thus far, it has worked. I am delighted to report that, just as at the University of Miami, no creature has been harmed in our canal-side training sessions.

The strategy, then, has been to use Shadow's active aggression to supply him with the discipline that will prevent the worst excesses of his reactive aggression from showing themselves. Unfortunately, it turned out to be a flawed strategy, certainly a limited one. I have come to realize that it is not possible to hide reactive aggression behind obedience, and the limitations of this attempt will be clearly displayed in certain situations – most notably close encounters. There is, for example, the annual humiliation at the local veterinarian's office. No amount of Platz, Sitz or Ici is going to help when people intrude this far into his orbit. So, when his annual check-up and boosters are due, I will drag in a markedly sedated and muzzled Shadow. 'Good morning, Doctor. Same plan as usual, I assume? I hold him, you stick him?'

Some would regard Shadow as a damaged dog, a defective example of the species. I don't see it that way. I think he is, instead, a very good example of a certain kind of dog: a deeply paranoid, distinctly dangerous East German working-line shepherd. This has certain advantages. As a few local Schutzhund trainers – whose dogs are temperamentally often not too dissimilar to Shadow – have said to me: *es Miami*. It's Miami. There is a fine line between a friendly dog and a stolen dog, and the one not infrequently becomes the other, especially when a dog with Shadow's level of obedience training can sell for upwards of $20K. Moreover, he loves his family with an intensity that I have seen in few other dogs. He would, I am convinced, protect us with his life. Nevertheless, my inability to solve the reactivity problem is a serious failure on my part – perhaps my biggest failure as a dog trainer. The result of my failure is that Shadow's life is much smaller than those of my former dogs. I feel sorry for him, and not a little guilty.

🐾

I used to take Shadow to dog parks when he was younger, before the testosterone had got to work on him and he started fighting every male dog he met and behaving in a generally unsavoury way towards their female counterparts. Even then, his territorialism was pronounced. If, for example, he decided that a bench was in his territory, he was going to mark it as such by urinating on it. If you happened to be sitting on this bench at that time, that wasn't going to slow him down at all. Three times Shadow did this. Three times in the space of a month.

Eventually, through this process of attrition – largely variations on the fighting, mating, urinating-on-people theme – the places that Shadow could advisably visit were slowly pruned. Our former dogs had been thoroughly integrated into our lives. If we went out to eat, we would make sure the restaurant was dog friendly. If we travelled – on vacation, sometimes even on business – our dog or dogs would come too. I once had a wolfdog, Brenin, who emigrated from the United States to Ireland with me, and then accompanied me around the various countries of Northern Europe. Then there was Nina, a German shepherd malamute mix, and Tess, Brenin's daughter, who were dual-country dogs, splitting their time between England and France, before finally retracing Brenin's steps back over the Atlantic. When I was on a book tour around parts of Europe in 2013, the whole family flew over from the United States with me, including Hugo, our German shepherd. On YouTube, you can see him sitting on the stage with me at some of my talks. (If it had been Shadow rather than Hugo, he would probably have spent this time formulating precise and individually tailored plans for how he was going to kill every single person in the audience.) Nor was that the first or last time Hugo flew to Europe. I am an autodidactic expert in getting large dogs from the United States to Europe and back again for summer holidays. It's not that expensive if you know how. I have stood with my dogs outside some of the best museums, monuments and galleries the world has to offer, leash in hand, while the other human members of the family improved themselves inside. All this has been denied Shadow because of his aggression. And because it has been denied Shadow it has been denied us too. Paranoid and dangerous he may be, but we love him, and are not going to deposit him in a kennel while we go away somewhere without him. That's assuming any kennel would take him, which is unlikely. Eating out and travelling have taken a temporary hiatus. Character is destiny. Heraclitus might have added to this by also noting that destinies are often entwined.

Shadow's reactive indiscretions have drastically diminished the boundaries of his world and decisively shaped the contours of the days of his life. The canal bank behind our house is one of the few remaining places left to him. I still run with him through the streets, when my knees are up to it. When they are not, Shadow might pull me on my bike through those same streets, churning out mile after mile. But the canal is the place he goes most because that is the only place where he can run unchained, run until his heart is ready to burst, and where he can express what he actively, aggressively and most truly is. If he couldn't do this, his soul would die. Character is destiny, and for no one is this truer than Shadow. This canal bank was waiting for Shadow his whole life, just as the rock of Sisyphus was waiting for him.

🐾

Shadow's reactive aggression has whittled away the limits of his world and brought him to this Lilliputian land of green iguanas and black vultures, Muscovy ducks and Egyptian geese, egrets and ibises, herons,

The Happiness of Dogs

snakes and turtles; manatees even, early in the morning. A fertile world, gratifyingly full of things to chase, but a small one nevertheless, and recognizably Sisyphean. These are the wages of his reactivity, but active aggression is just as much a part of Shadow as its reactive counterpart. In this active aggression, his life finds a kind of redemption. It is through his active aggression – directed towards iguanas or whatever local fauna happen to be available at the time – that he finds meaning even in this most Sisyphean of lives. Unlike Camus and Sisyphus, I don't need to *imagine* Shadow happy on this bank. His happiness is palpable. I can see it as clearly as I can see my hand. And unlike our alternative scenario of Sisyphus made happy by the gods intervening to change his attitude to his never-ending task, this is not a false happiness. It is not a happiness imposed on him from the outside or contrived by others. It is a happiness that stems from his innermost nature – a happiness that issues from what he essentially is, and that gives meaning to his Sisyphean labours. Meaning in life is not complicated. It is authentic happiness. That is all it is. Meaning in life arises when what you are and what you do coincide. It arises when there is not the slightest gap between identity and action; when there is nothing that separates what you are and what you do. Into such a gap doubt may insinuate itself. The resulting actions would not be pure but, rather, troubled. Shadow's actions are pure – as untainted as *les neiges d'antan*.

Shadow has shown how a life can be meaningful

even though it has no external point or purpose and aims only at repetition of itself. Although blissfully unaware that any such challenge existed, he has decisively answered the challenge of Sisyphus. The problem is that it is an answer only a dog can understand. Meaning comes effortlessly to Shadow's life, as easily as breathing. But our lives grow from meagre soils, and in ravines as barren as the boulders that litter their floors: difficult lands for meaning to take root. Meaning, for us, is a hard-won achievement, and one rarely attained. Judged in terms of the meaning it contains, Shadow's life eclipses mine.

It is this thought that motivates the pages to come. If this were merely a peculiarity of one or both of us – if Shadow's life were unusually meaningful or mine unusually meaningless – that would be interesting only as an oddity. But neither of us are outliers. As a general rule, I think, dogs lead more meaningful lives than we do. Working out why this is so – indeed, why it must be so – is what this book is all about.

2

The Unexamined Life

If I say again that the greatest good of man is daily to converse about virtue and the other things about which you hear me talking and examining myself and others, and that the life which is unexamined is not worth living – that you are still less likely to believe.

—Plato, *Apology*

Shadow soars like a bird into the air. And then he remembers that he is only a dog. Like Wile E. Coyote realizing he has run out of land, Shadow first looks down, and then plunges into the waiting canal beneath. He is still young in this memory – a couple of months short of his first birthday – not the old dog who sleeps at my feet as I write these words. In his attempted impersonation of a bird, Shadow is merely following in the footsteps, more pertinently the wing beats, of two real birds: brown Egyptian geese, who, fractions of a second before Shadow's leap, had wisely taken leave of the canal's western bank and now sit on its eastern counterpart. They appear to be vociferously voicing their disapproval of Shadow's behaviour. Or perhaps they are laughing at him. Egyptian geese talk a lot more than most other geese, and I have a feeling that much of what they have to say is rather negative.

The bank is near vertical, and the water is six feet down, probably nearer eight feet on this particular day as the canals have been drained in anticipation of Hurricane Irma's arrival in around thirty-six hours or so. A couple of days of putting up shutters are behind me, and a long exodus north lies in front of me, so I really don't have time for this. But Shadow is not getting out of there on his own. I am going to have to go down and haul him out by the scruff of his neck. Down the moccasin-snake-infested bank to the (albeit, only rarely) alligator-inhabited water below. It sounds awful but I'm used to it by now. He's not a year old yet, but we have already had this dance many times, my friend Shadow and me.

I love this memory because it is such a good example of a type of commitment that is possible only in a life that is gloriously unexamined. I can only admire Shadow's failure to compute even simple probabilities — such as what will happen if one keeps running when there is no ground left on which to run. Or perhaps he knows all too well what is going to happen and just doesn't care. Perhaps he even enjoys plunging into the canal. He certainly seems quite happy swimming around below me. But whatever is going on in his mind, one thing seems reasonably clear: dogs generally don't do self-examination. Compared with ours, the lives of dogs are resplendent in their lack of self-examination. We think this makes us better than them, makes our lives better than theirs. I suspect it is the other way around.

We think we are better because we can examine our lives and they can't, but this overlooks one salient fact: they don't need to examine their lives. That need is for creatures unlike them, creatures riddled with questions and, at the source of all questions, doubts. Taking leave of the earth, soaring into the sky, plunging into the depths: these are manifestations of a commitment that is deep and pure, unadulterated by doubt. In this commitment, there is not the slightest nook or fissure into which doubt may creep. This commitment is full, solid, an existential slab, hewn of granite. We humans, on the other hand, are creatures of doubt. It riddles us, like a cancer. Shadow's commitment is dense and solid, but ours is always hollow, diaphanous, as light as a feather.

The unexamined life is not worth living, Socrates said — or probably said. Most of what we think Socrates said were words put in his mouth by his student Plato, in a series of written dialogues in which Socrates was almost always the principal protagonist. This particular insight occurred in a dialogue called the *Apology*, which deals with the events surrounding Socrates' trial and death in 399 BC. Perhaps Socrates really said the things Plato says he said, or perhaps Plato was engaging in a little creative licence. It doesn't really matter. Whoever made this claim about the unexamined life seems to acknowledge that it is not particularly plausible (Socrates admits that it is something 'that you are still less likely to believe'). Curiously, however, there is no concerted attempt to provide any supporting evidence or argument. This claim seems to be less like the conclusion of a reasoned argument and more like an article of faith.

We should, however, cut Socrates a little slack. He was having a bad day. His fellow Athenians had recently found him guilty of corrupting the young and of not believing in the gods, and he was mulling over his preferred form of punishment. If he had any money, he mused, he might have proposed a fine. But pecuniary shortcomings left him with two options: exile or death. Exile, he thought, would have precluded the kind of self-examination that makes life worth living. Therefore, he chose death.

This is also curious. Why could Socrates not have uprooted his self-examination? Conducted it somewhere else? His reasons seem to be quite idiosyncratic and specific to Socrates' conception of what it was to examine one's life. Thinking, for Socrates, was something best done communally. Other people were centrally involved — essential foils — in his thinking and reasoning. (In this, Socrates was more like a dog than he might have realized — but that is a story for later.) When the Oracle of Delphi happened to mention that Socrates was the wisest man in Athens, he doubted this verdict and decided to prove her wrong. But he did this not, primarily, by turning his attention inwards and working out what he knew and didn't know. Instead, he asked others what they knew, or thought they knew, and then assessed whether they really did know what they thought they knew. (They didn't.) Socrates was, in his nature, a communal or social thinker. For Socrates, thinking was an activity most fruitfully done with others. For those of a more solitary persuasion, who find thinking a hard and painful undertaking, and consequently prefer to do their thinking alone, this is an alien mindset.

I don't know for sure why Socrates was this way, but I have a suspicion. Sometimes it seems to me that Socrates' behaviour bears the hallmarks of someone with little to no internal soliloquy: no tiny voice in his head with whom he could talk and generally think things through. This is ironic, as he claimed to have just such a voice – his *daemon* – which warned him against courses of action that would be detrimental to him. It is unclear what this daemon was doing in 399 BC, when the Athenians finally got around to condemning him to death. Doubly ironic would be the fact that the man who introduced the idea of the examined life may not have been particularly good at examining his own life. But sometimes we advocate not for how the world is but for how we would like it to be; legislate not for how we are but for how we would like ourselves to be. (Think, for example, of those 'family-values' politicians caught in the most un-family-values-like situations.) Self-legislation against those aspects of oneself that one does not like has a venerable history. It may be that Socrates' championing of the examined life was the result of a perceived deficit in himself.

Whether or not this is true, in pursuing his self-examination socially, Socrates styled himself the 'gadfly' of the Athenian people – a 'great and noble steed', but one that sometimes needed to be goaded into life; given to them by God, his mission was to awaken their intellectual and moral consciences and relieve them of their dogmas. The Athenian people, however, probably styled him in less flattering terms. Even though Athens was one of the most tolerant of the ancient Greek city states – it's perhaps significant that he didn't try the gadfly routine in Sparta, or even Thebes – the Athenians nevertheless sent him to the front line in various conflicts, including several battles in the Peloponnesian War (the battles of Amphipolis, Potidaea and Delium), where, as a hoplite, or infantryman, it was not unreasonable to suppose that he would have fallen on the battlefield. When that didn't happen – indeed, by all accounts, he distinguished himself as a soldier – the citizens of Athens eventually (it took them a few decades, but they got there in the end) concocted trumped-up charges and gave Socrates a choice: death or exile. Socrates chose death by hemlock. If the unexamined life is indeed not worth living, and if your self-examination is communal in nature, then exile and death would, for Socrates, have been largely equivalent. Might as well get it over with, Socrates reasoned, and so that's what he did. All of this for an unsupported article of faith.

🐾

Despite a dearth of supporting evidence and argument, and despite its acknowledged implausibility, the idea that the unexamined life is not worth living caught on. The idea became divorced from Socrates' peculiarly communal form of self-examination, and his notable emphasis on moral virtue became muted, although it did not disappear entirely. In subsequent centuries, self-examination became conceived of as an essentially individualistic phenomenon. What does it mean today to examine your life? Typically, as a largely solitary endeavour, it is one in which you ask yourself questions about your life. Questions such as:

Who am I?
How should I live?
What is the right thing to do?
Could I have done better?
Am I happy?
Should I be doing things differently?
How is my life going?
What do I want most in life?
Does my life have meaning?

This is not intended as an exhaustive list, and some of the questions, depending on how they are

The Unexamined Life

interpreted, will overlap with others. But I think it captures the general gist of what most people now have in mind when they think of examining their life.

In asking themselves questions of this sort, or other similar ones, people probably have, at least in the back of their mind, some idea of how to answer them. In trying to do so, they will probably bring to bear some principles that they happen to hold. It is difficult, for example, to answer the question 'What is the right thing to do?' without having some idea of the factors that make an action the right thing to do. It is difficult to judge whether your life has meaning without some idea of the factors that make life meaningful. Of course, these principles might also be questionable, necessitating a sort of meta-examination of the rules or principles you use to answer these questions about your life. And, in turn, these meta-principles might be questionable, necessitating a meta-meta-level investigation, and so on and so forth. Anything you can do I can do meta, as the old philosopher's joke goes.

So there are questions, and adjudications, and answerings, and meta-excursions, all focused squarely on the topic of one's life and what is going on in it. The result of all this interrogation – if done competently enough – is a suitably examined life. The sort of life of which Socrates might have approved, or at least not disapproved. Unfortunately, his approval could not have extended beyond the human species, for it is very likely that we are the only creatures that do this sort of thing. Are we to conclude, therefore, that the lives of all other creatures – present, past and future – have not been worth living? That seems a little harsh. Just the sort of thing, in fact, that a human would say.

Dogs don't do self-examination. Dogs can't ask the kind of questions listed above. Even if they could, they wouldn't have any idea where to begin answering them. If we take Socrates seriously, therefore, it seems we must conclude that the lives of dogs are not worth living. This claim would not just be true of the most unfortunate of dogs, forced to live lives of unremitting boredom or misery – of which there are, of course, far too many. Rather, since Socrates' claim is a general one, the inference we can draw is also general. If the unexamined life is not worth living, and if dogs do not examine their lives, then no dog's life has ever been worth living. Not even the lives of the happiest dogs – lives spent gambolling around cow pastures and returning home for delicious dinners and satisfied naps in front of the fire. That's what Socrates' claim seems to entail. Most, I assume, will find this entailment ridiculous. This is what is known as a *reductio ad absurdum*. If you have a theory or claim (e.g. the unexamined life is not worth living) and this theory or claim entails something absurd (e.g. the life of no dog has ever been worth living), then this theory or claim must also be absurd. Theories with absurd entailments are absurd theories.

Perhaps we might be more charitable to Socrates? We can rescue him from this charge of absurdity by restricting his claim to human lives: the unexamined

The Unexamined Life

human life is not worth living. This rids us of the ridiculous idea that the life of no dog – or of any other animal for that matter – has ever been worth living, but it risks introducing another human conceit. Humans, Socrates tells us, can do this great thing with their lives: examine them. So great is this thing that without it a human life is not worth living. But dogs never examine their lives. They can't. Given this juxtaposition, it is but a short step – and I know enough of Socrates to suspect it is a step he could not have resisted taking – to the idea that human lives are better than the lives of dogs. Human lives are better than the lives of dogs because we can and do examine our lives and they can't and don't examine theirs. We might grudgingly accept that their lives are worth living. But they are not as good as ours. Today, this is an entirely orthodox view – one held, I think, by a sizeable majority of humans. In the pages to follow, I am going to argue against it. Not only does examination make our lives no better than those of dogs; on balance, it probably makes them worse. Even in the case of humans, and certainly in the case of dogs, not only are unexamined lives worth living; often they are more worth living than their examined counterparts.

🐾

To ask any question about your life, and to attempt to answer it, you must be able to think about your life. What is your life? This is not as straightforward a question as it may seem, but for these preliminary purposes we can get away with some very general claims. At a bare minimum, your life is made up of you, what you do and why you do it. Your life is made up of you, your actions and the reasons for your actions. The latter category will comprise such things as thoughts, and feelings, beliefs, desires, hopes, fears, expectations, and many others. All of these fall under the rubric of what we might call mental acts. Calling them mental acts does not assume they are non-physical. Mental acts might be the same thing as brain processes, for example, in which case they would be as physical as anything else. Drawing these threads together, we might think of your life as made up of you and what you do: you and your acts, whether these are bodily acts or mental ones. If so, then to think about your life is to think about yourself and your bodily and mental acts. The ability to do this goes by different names, but I am going to call it *reflection*. Reflection is a form of self-awareness (although as we shall see later, it is important to understand that it is not the only form). Reflection is the ability to think about yourself, and about your life. It is the ability to think about the various things you do, and all the reasons you have for doing them.

Many mental acts, perhaps all, have what is, when you think about it, a rather remarkable feature: they are about things. Seeing, for example, is a basic mental act. If I see Shadow running, then Shadow is the object of my seeing; it is what my seeing is about. I see him.

The Unexamined Life

But so too is his running. I see this too. I see Shadow running. This is what my act of seeing is about. I see also the Egyptian geese standing at the very edge of the bank and see that Shadow is running at breakneck speed towards them. On seeing this, I think that this is likely to end badly – that Shadow will soon be taking a plunge into the canal. Thinking is another type of mental act. In this case, Shadow's impending plunge into the canal is what my thought is about. It is, as philosophers often put it, the content of my thought. The content of a mental act is what that act is about. Shadow's running is the content of my act of seeing. That Shadow will be taking an imminent plunge into the canal is the content of my resulting act of thinking.

In reflection, a mental act turns back on its owner. You become the content of your mental acts. If you see yourself in a mirror, you are the content of your act of seeing. We even talk here of seeing your 'reflection'. But reflection as I am using that concept is broader than this. Reflection occurs whenever a mental act of yours turns back on you or some aspect of you – so that you become the content of that act. On seeing yourself in the mirror, you might think, 'I look great!' Or you might think, 'I need to lose a few pounds.' Both of these are thoughts about you: you are the content of these thoughts. Therefore, they are also cases of reflection as I am using this concept.

There are many varieties of mental acts. Not only can you see yourself and think about yourself, you can have wishes or hopes regarding yourself. You can have dreams about your future life. You can have expectations about yourself and your future conduct. You can remember things that happened to you, or things that you once did. You can imagine yourself in various situations, including ones you know will never happen. Seeing, thinking, hoping, wishing, wanting, expecting, remembering and imagining are all examples of mental acts, and there are many more besides these. When these mental acts have you as their content – when they are in some way or other about you – then they are all cases of reflection. The visual case, where we talk of seeing your 'reflection' in a mirror, is just the most basic example of this much broader category of reflection.

In reflection, your mental acts turn back on you. You become the content of those acts. However, reflection also occurs when it is not you, but some part or facet of you, that becomes the content of one of your mental acts. You might look in the mirror and focus not on you *in toto*, but on, say, your face. You can, for example, think not just about yourself but about that irregular freckle you really should get checked out. One particularly important form of reflection is the ability to focus on your mental acts themselves – on what you are thinking, or feeling, on what you want to do next, on your hopes, dreams and fears. That thought is troubling. That feeling is puzzling. That memory is comforting. Reflection occurs when your mental acts turn back either on you or on some part or facet of you, a part or facet that you recognize as yours, whether this is mental or physical.

The Unexamined Life

Reflection – especially when focused on your own mental acts – is a complicated ability. But it is not as complicated an ability as self-examination. Rather, reflection is what makes self-examination possible. To get self-examination you would need to add to reflection some quite sophisticated cognitive abilities – the ability to think and reason with a certain level of proficiency. But without the capacity for reflection, you will not be able to direct these reasoning powers on yourself. Without reflection you would not be able to even ask the kinds of questions listed earlier, let alone answer them. Reflection is a pre-condition of the examined life – a necessary but not sufficient condition of self-examination. If Socrates is right and the unexamined life is not worth living, reflection is a necessary condition of a life worth living. A life without the capacity for reflection is a life not worth living.

Socrates is undeniably – and justifiably – regarded as one of the principal architects of Western thought. There is, however, another, rather different, strand of Western thought which takes a notably less positive view of the value of reflection. When Adam and Eve ate the apple of the tree of knowledge of good and evil, they became aware of themselves for the first time. How do we know this? Because, we are told, they were now ashamed of their nakedness, and hastened off in search of some suitably sized fig leaves. Shame is only possible for a creature capable of reflection. Shame is shame in the eyes of a nominal other – whether that other is someone else, or you, or some non-existent alternative.

The Happiness of Dogs

In this case, the other was, of course, God. In shame you understand, or think you understand, how you appear to this other. The story of the Fall, then, is a story of the advent of reflection. Neither Adam and Eve nor their God seemed to regard this as a good thing. God banished Adam and Eve from the Garden of Eden, and they henceforth had to face all the hardships of the world. He even put an angel with a flaming sword on guard duty to make sure they didn't try to sneak back in. God's judgement seems unequivocal: it would have been better if this capacity for reflection had never been born in humans.

To my great surprise, on this matter I am inclined to side with God over Socrates, with the Bible over the *Apology*. Of course, I realize that reflection, together with the resulting ability to examine one's life, brings undoubted benefits. Humans – what marvellous creatures we are, with our meticulously examined lives. However, this is not a book about the benefits of being human; rather, it is a book about its drawbacks. Specifically, it is book about the drawbacks of a certain, quintessentially human, trait. It is about the cost of the examined life and, in particular, the cost of the capacity that makes such a life possible: reflection.

🐾

Existence – human existence included – is a game of swings and roundabouts. Reflection is a capacity that developed during human evolution, and any developed

The Unexamined Life

capacity has its costs as well as its benefits. When the capacities are exclusively human or strongly associated with being human, then we (humans) tend to focus on the benefits, especially when these are significant and multifarious. It is difficult to keep one's eye on the costs, especially when these are less obvious.

Consider two examples of developments of this sort — developments with obvious benefits but more subtle costs. The first: brains. Who could possibly take issue with brains, with all the many and varied benefits they bring? Surely brains can't be regarded as anything but an unqualified success? The humble sea squirt, however, takes a different view. In its juvenile days, shortly after it is born, a sea squirt spends its time swimming around near the seabed. At that time in its life, the sea squirt is a chordate, the phylum that includes mammals, birds, reptiles and fish. This is because it has certain anatomical features that are definitive of this group, including a rudimentary spine (the notochord) and brain (the cerebral ganglion), and these allow it to navigate its way along the seabed. Upon reaching the age of maturity, however, the sea squirt will anchor itself to the seabed, and then it will begin a remarkable transformation. It absorbs the tail that formerly propelled it, the primitive eye that allowed it to see, its primitive spina notochord, and finally, its rudimentary brain. It is now no longer a chordate but 'merely' a tunicate. In essence, it eats the features that made it the former. It eats, among other things, its own brain. (This, as the neuroscientist Rodolfo Llinás once quipped, is rather like when an academic is awarded tenure at a university.)

You might ask: why not keep the brain? Brains are generally good things to have. So if you already have one, why not keep it? Ditto for the eye and spine. The vicissitudes of fortune being what they are, you never know when you might need them again. Perhaps your anchorage point wasn't as good as it looked? You might need to move. The answer is that even things with undeniable benefits, such as brains, have their associated costs. Brains require energy to maintain – energy that can't then be used for other purposes, such as feeding and, the acid test of any evolutionary development, reproduction. A brain, fundamentally, is a biological strategy, and any strategy stands or falls on the relative weight of its costs and benefits. Sometimes, in certain circumstances, the costs of brains can outweigh their benefits.

Here is another example: writing. Who could overlook the benefits of this immensely important cultural development? Information that we formerly needed to store in our brain we can now externalize in an information-bearing store outside ourselves. We can avail ourselves of this information as needed: once we learn to read, we can tap into a potentially unlimited store of information. Unlike the brain, which has limited storage capacity, this external information-bearing store that is written language has no limits on storage and is typically more robust and permanent than the brain. Human civilization, in anything remotely resembling its current form, would not have been possible without the development of writing. The benefits are large, and obvious. But this does not alter the fact that the development of writing also had its costs. In a classic study conducted early in the twentieth century, Russian psychologists Alexander Luria and Lev Vygotsky identified some of these costs. In preliterate cultures, much of the burden of remembering is placed on natural, biological memory. For example, aboriginal cultures, they reported, can remember song cycles that last several nights. With the development of literacy, this outstanding natural memory tends to wither. The same pattern is found developmentally, where eidetic – or photographic – memory is far more common in children than in adults. Evolution, Luria and Vygotsky argue, is also *involution* – the withering away of newly vestigial forms.

A dog exists differently to a human. It exists in a different way. The philosophical study of the ways in which things exist is known as *existential phenomenology*. This discipline only studies the existence of some things – things that are conscious. In fact, existential phenomenologists use the term 'existence' in a technical way that restricts it to beings that are conscious. Only conscious beings exist in this sense. Non-conscious things – tables, chairs, clouds, cabbages, etc. – can have *being*, but only conscious creatures *exist*. The goal of existential phenomenology is to understand the fundamental structures of consciousness by virtue of which a conscious creature exists in the specific way that it does.

Reflection is a fundamental structure of consciousness — it is, in effect, consciousness turning back on itself. Reflection is thinking about thinking, thinking about thoughts, and about the thinker of those thoughts. Creatures that can do this — and, as we shall see shortly, the capacity for reflection is far more widespread and pronounced in humans than in any other creature — will exist in a different way than creatures that cannot. This difference in a way of existing will have certain benefits, but also certain drawbacks or deficits.

The deficits appear to us in our lives and in many forms. But the fundamental form is just what we would expect both from the story of the Fall and from the basic structure of reflection. Reflection is what we might think of as an agent of separation. It is akin to a spotlight shone on a stage that picks out one person from all the others, demarcating and separating this person from those others. Reflection is consciousness turning back on itself. But to turn back on itself is, at the same time, to turn away from the world. Reflection is consciousness turning inwards rather than outwards towards the world. Reflection pulls us out of the world and into ourselves.

The story of the Fall picks up on one consequence of this focus. The story of the Fall is about losing one's home. With their banishment from the Garden, Adam and Eve lost their home. They were forced to find a home in another place, far less welcoming. They never felt quite at home in this new, harsher world, and their remaining years were ones of bitter regret. The story, therefore, seeks to communicate an important message about the human condition. We are creatures of reflection. As such, our fundamental condition is, as Martin Heidegger once put it, *unheimlich*. Literally, this means scary, or eerie. But *heim* means 'home'. Our lives are eerie in the sense that we have no real home. We are unhomed creatures: never quite at home in the world, never quite comfortable in our skins any more.

Deep down, I think we recognize the baleful effects of reflection. Why else would we spend so much of our lives trying to get away from it? After a long day at work, I might return home and say, 'I don't want to think about anything tonight.' What I really mean is that I don't want to think about myself. For a human, thinking about anything at all quickly opens the door to reflection. Thinking about work cannot be separated from thinking about how I did at work, about what I could have done better, about what I should do when I go back to work in the morning. We humans think and we think, but soon it all turns back to us. The self is quickly inserted into all our thinking, no matter what it is about. For an adult human, except in comparatively rare circumstances, to think at all is to think about yourself. It is not the thinking one hates. It is the fact that one is in it.

The role played by reflection in the finest of our human achievements is well known. But while reflection may be essential to human distinctiveness, some of the highest and best human endeavours can only occur when reflection has bid us farewell, if only for a while. We tell ourselves that our painting, our sculpture, our music, our literature – the finest of human artistic achievements, and found in no other creature – would be impossible without reflection. Perhaps this is true. However, it is noticeable that the highest expressions of these art forms occur in the absence of reflection. There is the virtuoso concert pianist lost in the Liszt sonata she is playing. There is the novelist having one of those mornings where the words flow, as if with a strange life of their own, from his keyboard. There is the artist lost in her painting, oblivious to everything else. The highest expressions of human creativity are *flow* experiences in the sense coined by Mihaly Csikszentmihalyi. These are precisely experiences where the reflective sense of self is at its most attenuated.

Perhaps the greatest indicator of the value we place on the absence of reflection is in our love of sport, found in almost all cultures. Anyone who has played a sport with any degree of competence knows that flow is essential here too – that success in athletic endeavours occurs most often when reflection has been temporarily banished. In this sense, sports take us back to a time before the Fall, when we were creatures untainted by reflection. When we play, and all is going right, and we flow from one movement into the next, never thinking about ourselves and what we are doing, because we

The Unexamined Life

know thinking would be flow's death, that is when we are most like our dogs.

Reflection, most fundamentally, is a wound that cannot be healed. It neatly severs us in two, and has left us uneasy, troubled creatures. However strong our desire to become what we want to be, and however many decades of endeavour we put into its service, what we most want to be we can never be – for we can never again simply be anyone or anything. Our lives are futile spasms. We suffer anguish in the face of our freedom to choose and alienation in the face of our choices. We find love so difficult. If we think about our lives at all, using our vaunted capacity for reflection, we quickly realize they don't make sense: as if the price we had to pay for understanding our lives was realizing their absurdity. Reflection, and not Uriel, is the true name of the angel with the flaming sword who stands on the eastern gate of Eden.

Think of the human mind as the land after Eden. Think of it as the place where Adam and Eve were forced to live after their exile. This is a land dominated by a canyon, broad and deep, and the name of this canyon is Reflection. This is our home now, as barren as boulders. We were not, however, sent to face the hardships of this world alone. With us came a creature, like us in many ways – similar enough for us to spend our lives side by side – but whose capacity for reflection is, compared with ours, nascent at best. A vast canyon in us, reflection in this creature is merely a vague indentation in the sand; a suggestion of something deeper, but no more than this. The consciousness of this creature is undivided, unbroken and, consequently, the creature exists in a very different way from us. I have just pulled such a creature from the water, and will shortly load him into a Jeep for our long exodus north, running from Irma. What would normally be a four-hour drive to Orlando will take us twenty. He is going to smell of canal the entire way. Another one of these creatures may be lying at your feet as you read these words. Or perhaps lying next to you on a couch. Perhaps he is sitting next to you, eyes boring into you, petitioning for a morning walk. We share our lives with these creatures and are, therefore, well placed to learn from them. We might even regard them as instructors, although they are peculiar ones since they don't understand the lessons they impart. They have no need of such lessons. But I suspect that we do. These creatures are a guide to a type of existence that is alien to ours, but in some ways better. This, I believe, is a learning opportunity that we cannot afford to ignore.

3

Mirror, Mirror

> Nothingness lies coiled in the heart of being –
> like a worm.
>
> —Jean-Paul Sartre, *Being and Nothingness*

The ability to recognize oneself in a mirror forms the basis of a well-known research programme in comparative and developmental psychology, initially conceived by the psychologist Gordon Gallup in 1970. In the mirror test, a mark (typically dye) is placed on an animal (ideally when anesthetized) in a position where it is visible only in a mirror. If the animal, upon waking, uses the mirror to inspect the mark, then it is deemed to recognize that the body reflected in the mirror is its own. And implicit in this recognition is the ability to think thoughts about itself, thoughts such as, 'Yup, that's me.' This mirror test, therefore, is a test for what I have called *reflection*. Specifically, it tests for the ability to visually identify, and thereby think thoughts about, oneself – one of the forms that reflection can take. (As we shall see shortly, there is another form, less widely recognized, but equally important.) This form of reflection has featured prominently in the history of philosophy. The eighteenth-century German philosopher Immanuel Kant called it empirical apperception. Jean-Paul Sartre labelled it positional or reflective self-awareness. Contemporary philosophers often prefer to talk of self-reference. None of these locutions are notably mellifluous. In calling it reflection, I have opted for a simpler variant.

Reflection, as explained earlier, is the ability to make oneself, or some part or facet of oneself, into the content of one's own mental acts. I can do this by thinking about myself, or by remembering something I did, or by having hopes for my future. I can do it in various ways, but perhaps the most basic of these is by recognizing myself in the mirror. When I do, I am the content of my own act of seeing – I am what I see. Subsequent thoughts I might think – 'That's me' being the most obvious – are also examples of reflection. Reflection is a form of self-awareness where my own mental acts are directed towards me. The capacity for reflection, therefore, is what the mirror test tests for.

Reflection is a form of self-consciousness, and is not the same as consciousness or awareness per se. (I shall use the terms 'consciousness' and 'awareness' interchangeably.) Much of the time, probably most of the time unless one is extraordinarily self-absorbed, our consciousness is directed towards things other than us. For obvious reasons, if we step out into the road our attention is on the bus that might hit us; in other situations it might be on the project with the impending deadline, or on what to have for dinner this evening. Consciousness is typically other-directed, rather than self-directed. If it wasn't, we might not last very long. The mirror test does not test for other-directed consciousness, only for the self-directed variant. Therefore, it is not a test for consciousness in general. It does not demarcate animals that are conscious from animals that are not; at most, it only distinguishes animals that are conscious of themselves from animals that are not. I mention this only because Gallup, in his articulation of the significance of the mirror test, was confused about this, and his confusion was inherited by more than a few.

It is not entirely clear which animals pass the mirror test, partly because the number of species thus far tested is rather low. It is generally accepted that humans (over the age of eighteen to twenty-four months), chimpanzees, bonobos and orangutans consistently pass the test. Gorillas, to be quite frank, have struggled, although this is probably because they regard eye contact as an aggressive gesture, and so avoid looking at each other's faces – including faces that stare back at them in a mirror. Other animals that seem to pass the test – although some dispute this – include elephants, dolphins and pigeons. Among fish, manta rays and wrasse have been patiently building their cases too.

Dogs, on the other hand, struggle with the test. That may appear strange. I would hate to be guilty of pisceanophobia – the word I think I might have just made up for anti-fish prejudice – but to me it would be quite surprising if wrasse turned out to be self-aware creatures while dogs didn't. However, perhaps it's not that strange that dogs don't do well with the test, and it has nothing to do with lack of reflection, or self-awareness, but much more to do with the average dog's utter lack of concern for how he or she looks in a mirror. The world of dogs is a world of smells as much as it is of sights, and in general they seem to care far more about the former than the latter.

🐾

I spent much of my thirties in splendid isolation – in lonely, yet often lovely, solitude. At that time, my immediate family – defined as family living in the same country as me – was an exclusively canine one. I lived with three dogs. Brenin was a wolfdog – a wolf probably mixed with giant malamute. In this memory, he is seven years old and in his pomp. A hillocky canine bull – thirty-five inches at the withers and weighing nearly 150 pounds. Middle age has perhaps softened him a little, and the 135 pounds of previous years would have been a better weight for him. But here, in this memory, he is still magnificent. Nina is his friend, eighty-five pounds of stocky and pugnacious German shepherd alloyed with malamute. Tess is Brenin's daughter. Like Nina, Tess weighs around eighty-five pounds, but she is taller and noticeably more willowy. In some ways she is the image of her father, but her coat is grey instead of Brenin's brown.

In this memory, we have just returned from our daily run through the fields and woodlands of the Rathmore peninsula, outside Kinsale, on the south coast of Ireland. The three of them lie sprawled in the living room in front of the cast-iron log burner. Collectively they take up almost the entire room, a gigantic fur triptych that spreads from wall to wall. And beyond this room, there isn't a lot of house left. Tess has slightly distanced herself from the others, being the recent recipient of a telling-off and hosing-down from me. (Even now I am still muttering curses under my breath.) She still reeks heavily of cow dung. This is far from an unusual occurrence.

I loved Brenin like a brother. He had many fine qualities, but affability towards other dogs was not among them. Indeed, he harboured a murderous hostility towards any male dog above a certain size and age. Nina adopted essentially the same stance towards female dogs. Thus, between the two of them, I could expect a homicidal antipathy being directed towards practically any dog we met on our daily excursions. To ensure the safety of the peninsula's dog population, meagre though it was, our daily walks were governed by an unbreakable edict. Brenin, Nina and Tess could go anywhere they wanted, as long as it was behind me. It was a rule targeted at Brenin and Nina, not Tess, who delighted in the presence of other dogs and became intensely excited whenever she met one. But there was no way on earth Brenin and Nina would agree to stay behind me if Tess didn't, and so the rule applied to all three. *Anywhere behind, nowhere in front* was a rule that had been drummed into them day in and day out for most of their lives. If we encountered a dog, I would make a rapid assessment of its gender and grab the appropriate member of the pack. A few unfortunate episodes aside – all of them cases of gender misidentification – the procedure worked well.

While clearly necessary, the *anywhere behind, nowhere in front* rule had one unfortunate consequence. Ironically, this involved Tess, the only one who didn't need the rule. While amiable towards other dogs, Tess had a very different attitude towards other species. She was lightning fast, fast as a striking snake, and she took her hunting very seriously. Rats would do – she would dispense death with minimal fuss – but rats were easy to catch. Her favourites were the much faster, semi-ubiquitous rabbits we encountered every day. To rabbits, Tess was the devil incarnate, the terror of the earth. She didn't manage to kill many – something for which I was very grateful – but she did dispatch some. And whether death was the ultimate result or not, each day she approached hunting with admirable vigour, rigour, and an enthusiasm that was always undimmed by failure. Perhaps this highly developed prey drive was the reason she developed the nasty habit of rolling in cow dung. Sheep dung would have sufficed, but the fields surrounding our house were generally rented by dairy farmers. Since Tess was subsumed under the

Mirror, Mirror

anywhere behind, nowhere in front rule, and since I did not have eyes in the back of my head, this meant she had ample opportunities to engage in her passion.

One theory is that dogs roll in dung to mask their scent when they hunt. Whether this was the reason Tess did it or not, she was a recidivist offender. Picture her as I do now, returning to our little cottage suitably chastened by the stern lecture she has received from me, and understanding that there is a hosing coming her way. This picture is a useful portrayal of what motivates Tess and what does not. Tess is clearly motivated by smells. For some reason, she wants to smell like cow dung. Perhaps she has a good reason for this, perhaps not. Either way, the desire to smell like this seems, for her, to be highly motivating. She does it all the time, and even the looming threat of a hosing – which she detests – does not deter her. What almost certainly does not motivate her, however, is the issue of how she looks in a mirror.

Sometimes when an animal fails a psychological test set by us humans, its failure is not so much because it can't pass the test but because it can't be bothered to pass it. Motivation is often crucial to whether an animal passes the test, and dogs are particularly susceptible to motivational failures. If a dog does not react to its image in a mirror – does not inspect a dye mark that has appeared on it, for example – this is quite likely to be because it doesn't care about how it looks in a mirror.

The problem of motivation, and the resulting limitations of the mirror test, have become widely recognized by scientists working on self-awareness in animals. It is a vision-orientated test, and it only works with animals that are suitably motivated by visual cues. Living in a world of smells as much as sights, dogs are far more interested in dung than in how they look in the mirror. The same is true – perhaps even more so – of the heady aroma of urine. This has led to the development of interesting olfactory variants on the mirror test. Inspired by this idea, for example, biologist Marc Bekoff ran an impromptu experiment that, for reasons that will shortly become obvious, became known colloquially as the *yellow snow test*. Living in Boulder, Colorado, where there is plenty of snow around, Marc recorded how long his dog Jethro spent sniffing urine – his own and others' – in the snow. To make sure Jethro couldn't identify his own urine by remembering where he deposited it, Marc shovelled up Jethro's yellow snow and moved it to new locations. Jethro, Marc recorded, spent significantly less time sniffing his own relocated urine than he did sniffing the urine of other dogs – suggesting he could differentiate between urine that was his from urine that was not.

Does this show that Jethro has a concept of 'mine' and, therefore, the related concept of 'me'? That he is, in other words, capable of reflection, in the form of thoughts of the sort 'This urine is *mine*' or 'This came from *me*'? The ability to think 'me' or 'mine' thoughts is a form of reflection. Alas, however, there are other possible explanations. Perhaps Jethro merely discriminates yellow snow that is 'more interesting' from yellow snow that is 'less interesting'; he is driven to pay more attention to some patches of yellow snow over others without understanding why. This is known as a problem of *stimulus equivalence*. According to this deflationary hypothesis, all cases of uninteresting yellow snow are cases of his own urine, and all cases of his own urine are also cases of uninteresting yellow snow. Therefore, we can't determine to which feature – that of his-ownness or that of uninterestingness – Jethro is responding.

We can see the same distinction in possible explanations of Tess's dung-rolling behaviour. Before a good roll, did Tess think to herself, '*I* shall roll in this dung to mask *my* scent'? This is an 'I/my' thought, and if she can think 'I' or 'my' thoughts, she is capable of reflection. Or did she simply find herself inexplicably attracted to cow dung and enjoyed rolling in it without understanding why? Both might equally facilitate her hunting endeavours, assuming that's why she did it. As far as her scent-masking hunting strategy is concerned, what matters is that she rolls in cow dung and not why she rolls in it. On the first interpretation, Tess is capable of reflection: she can think thoughts about *herself* (*I* shall roll in the dung) or about something that is *hers* (*my* scent). The second interpretation entails no such thing. It just turned out that, for reasons she could not fathom, she found the cow dung alluring. If so, there is no need for her to think any thoughts about herself. All she need do is find some dung and commence rolling. The moral is that wishing to mask her scent and being attracted to the pungent aroma of dung could, in principle, yield the same behaviour in Tess – namely, rolling in it. Therefore, this behaviour can't be used to establish the truth of one hypothesis over the other.

Alexandra Horowitz of Barnard College has perhaps done more ingenious things with dog urine than anyone else in the world. Building on the work of Roberto Gatti at Tomsk State University, she devised an experiment with a view to solving this problem of stimulus equivalence. The first step involved gathering thirty-six dogs (all of which, being dogs, were presumably urine aficionados). Then the experiment was divided into three trials involving three canisters. In every trial there was one canister that had only water in it. That was the control canister. The contents of the other two containers varied with each trial. In the first trial, one canister contained a given dog's urine, and the other contained that dog's urine modified with an added scent. In the second trial, one canister contained the dog's urine and the other the urine of an unfamiliar dog. In the third trial, one canister had the dog's urine with an added scent and the other the added scent alone. Horowitz found that the dogs spent more time sniffing their modified urine and the urine of other dogs than their own unmodified urine. In fact, judged by the time they spent sniffing it, their own modified urine seemed about as interesting to the dogs as the urine of other dogs.

Does this solve the problem of stimulus equivalence – of working out whether dogs are responding to the interestingness or to the otherness of the urine? Not by itself. It could be that the dogs simply found their own modified urine interesting – without recognizing that it was their own urine that had been modified. To address this concern, Horowitz added an extra step in the experiment (this extra step was only undergone by twelve dogs rather than by the original total of thirty-six, so the sample class was very small). If the dogs found the modified urine interesting without realizing it was their own urine that had been modified, why would this be? It must be, Horowitz reasoned, because they found the added scent interesting. So what we can do is test the dog's interest in the added scent – in this case, anise oil. Horowitz found that, as expected, the dogs spent more time examining their modified urine than their unmodified counterpart. However, they also spent more time investigating their modified urine than the anise oil alone. This, Horowitz argues, suggests it is the modification of their own odour that the dogs found interesting rather than the modifying odour itself.

Ingenious undoubtedly; brilliant possibly. But does it solve the original problem? I'm not sure it does. A committed fan of the problem of stimulus equivalence could always claim that it is when anise oil and the dog's own urine are added together that the interest kicks in. On their own, one might claim, they are both largely uninteresting – it's only when you add them together that the magic happens and, crucially, the dog can still be interested in the combination without understanding why. I don't know. Perhaps it is not possible to devise experiments that will solve the problem of stimulus equivalence and thus show, beyond all doubt, that dogs pass the olfactory version of the mirror test. Perhaps it is. My concerns lie elsewhere.

These concerns can be stated bluntly: *How did we get here?* To this point in logical space, that is. I started talking about dung several pages ago. Urine worked its way into the conversation a little later. Thus, an unsympathetic critic might allege that I have spent the past few pages essentially *talking shit* and *taking the piss*.

Understood as a test for self-awareness, the mirror test faces two severe limitations. The first limitation is that, whether they are conducted in visual or in olfactory form, mirror self-recognition tests test for only one form of self-awareness, the form that I have called reflection. This is the ability to think thoughts about oneself, thoughts such as 'Yes, that's me' when presented with your reflection in a mirror, or 'Yes, that's mine' when presented with a pile of yellow snow. There is another form of self-awareness, equally important if not more so, that cannot be tested for in this way. This form of self-awareness also puts in appearances at various junctures in the history of philosophy. Kant called it transcendental apperception. Sartre called it pre-reflective awareness, or non-positional self-awareness, or non-thetic self-awareness. In certain circles – those of late-twentieth-century analytic philosophy (the circles, in other words, in which I cut my philosophical teeth) – you might hear it described as self-awareness that is immune to error through misidentification. I shall call it *pre-reflection*. A creature capable of pre-reflection is necessarily aware of itself, but pre-reflectively rather than reflectively. Even if dogs don't pass the mirror test, or its olfactory counterpart, they can still be aware of themselves in this second, pre-reflective, sense. In fact, it is almost impossible for them not to be aware of themselves in this second sense because, as we shall see shortly, pre-reflection is built into any conscious experience. Any animal – human, canine or otherwise – that is conscious of the world at all will be pre-reflectively aware of itself too.

The second limitation of the mirror test has to do with its role in testing for reflection. Reflection can take different forms. One form is bodily self-recognition, and the mirror test, at least for animals who care how they look in a mirror, can be thought of as testing for this. However, reflection comes in another form: the ability to think about one's mental states rather than about one's body – to think about what one is thinking, and feeling, about what one wants, hopes, fears, expects and dreads. Whether it is carried out in visual or olfactory form, the mirror test clearly does not test for this sort of ability. So the mirror test begins to look rather restricted. First, there is another form of self-awareness — pre-reflection — for which it does not test at all. And second, even if we restrict ourselves to reflection, it turns out to test for only one of its forms. I shall discuss each of these points in turn.

To see what the idea of pre-reflection amounts to, let us jump forward in time again, to Shadow and his saga-like vendetta against the iguanas — the *Skugga Saga*, as my Icelandic acquaintances might label it. Shadow's visual identification of an iguana seems to be based on identification via silhouette. I say this because Shadow can make mistakes. Sometimes, various palm fronds and other tree detritus will be arranged in such a way that they look, from a distance, like an iguana. That is, they present an iguana-like silhouette. After his initial northerly and southerly sallies, Shadow will calm down, and whenever he sees what he takes to be an iguana he will stalk it. If there is no iguana there, there will come a point in his stalking when he realizes this, and breaks off back to his happy, bouncing trot. On the other hand, if it is an iguana, the stalking will continue until the iguana breaks cover and Shadow bursts into chase.

From this we can conclude that Shadow sees some silhouettes as iguanas, and there may or may not be an iguana there. He does not think of them as iguanas in the way we do, of course. He does not know that they are reptiles, that they are vertebrates, that they are cold-blooded and so on. Rather, he presumably sees and thinks of them in affordance-based terms. The idea of an affordance comes from the perceptual psychologist James Gibson. The affordances of an object are what the object offers the creature that sees it – whether good or bad. For Brenin, male dogs above a certain size and age afforded fighting, and female dogs afforded the same thing for Nina. For Tess, dung afforded rolling in. For Shadow, iguanas afford one of his favourite things in the world: chasing. Iguanas are for him, fundamentally, *chaseable* things. Perhaps he makes distinctions within the category of chaseable things. Perhaps he distinguishes chaseable things that go up, such as ducks, from chaseable things that go down (into the canal) – namely, iguanas. Perhaps he distinguishes chaseable things that go up into the air (ducks again) from chaseable things that go up into trees (squirrels). It would make sense for Shadow to draw these distinctions because his hunting strategy depends on them. But let's work with the general category of the chaseable.

Shadow sees iguanas as chaseable things. But he also sometimes sees arboreal detritus as chaseable – before he realizes his mistake. This moment of realization is important because it reveals something crucial about the nature of vision. Seeing is a *predictive* process. This idea was central to the phenomenological tradition in philosophy, instigated by Edmund Husserl and continued, in the form of existential phenomenology, by Martin Heidegger, Jean-Paul Sartre and Maurice Merleau-Ponty, among others. It has recently been revived in the *predictive-processing* account of vision which understands the visual brain as a predictive machine, continually making guesses about what is causing current perceptions and adjusting and updating those guesses as further information comes in.

I was given a crash course in the predictive nature of vision some years ago. After Brenin died, I had a series of strange experiences that lasted some months, perhaps even years. If I woke up in the middle of the night, I would sometimes see him standing by the side of the bed, next to me in the dark. Distinctly spooky, but at the same time mundane: it is a straightforward consequence of the way the visual brain works. Vision is prediction. To see is to predict. The brain – specifically the visual cortex – is an inveterate guesser. In the dark of my bedroom, my brain was doing its best to see – trying to make sense of the patterns of shapes and shadows it was presented with by coming up with its best guess of what was causing them. Since Brenin had been such a huge part of my life for eleven years, he featured prominently in these guesses. He would appear next to me in the dark because my visual brain guessed he was there. And it guessed he was there because, when he was alive, he probably would have been. It wasn't an unreasonable guess for the visual cortex, which doesn't have access to general, non-visual facts, such as Brenin's demise; it was merely incorrect. The result of this guess was a quasi-visual experience that, for a moment or two, was difficult to distinguish from a true, veridical experience. But then Brenin would dissolve in front of my eyes, breaking down into twinkling motes of visual dust that slowly dimmed and darkened and became part of the night.

Brenin wasn't there, but the iguanas certainly are. Shadow sees an iguana, or sees some tree debris as an iguana, because his brain has made guesses about how his future experiences will unfold in the event of certain things happening. The event of certain things happening is what is known as a *contingency*, and how future experiences unfold is a *consequence* of this contingency. Shadow's visual brain has made various guesses about the relation between contingencies and consequences. For example, the first contingency: Shadow continues to slowly approach, swinging to his left to approach from behind. The resulting consequence: the side of the iguana slowly disappears, and its long tail comes into view. The second contingency: Shadow charges. The resulting consequence: the side profile of the iguana (body, head and tail) moves rapidly as the iguana darts down the bank, splashing into the canal. As you can imagine, there is an indefinite number of potential contingency–consequence pairings; these two merely scratch the surface. Shadow can see the iguana because he has anticipated at least some of these pairings.

It is prediction, or expectation, that provides the link between contingencies and consequences. But sometimes there can be a violation of expectations. Perhaps, when Shadow moves behind the object, the long tail of the iguana does not appear. Instead, there is only a lump of tree bark. Shadow breaks his stalk and charges. Instead of the expected explosive leap into the canal, the object remains resolutely in place. Seeing is predicting, and violations of predictions cause you to revise your predictions and thereby change what it is you see.

Now comes the crucial step in the argument: the step that takes us from prediction to pre-reflection. Shadow is implicated in many of the predictions he makes when he sees something as an iguana. What is crucial in this continuing dance of contingencies and consequences is not that a dog has changed its coordinates in visual space, nor that an iguana has changed its position. Rather, it is crucial that they have moved in this way relative to each other. What is important is not that the iguana moves to this position, or that position, or changes its position in Cartesian space – like a GPS location pin on a phone. Rather, as far as the unfolding of Shadow's future experiences go, what is crucial is that the iguana moves in this or that way relative to Shadow. If the iguana moves, say, three feet to the north, then precisely what consequences this will have for Shadow's future experiences depends on where Shadow is. If he is standing to the east, for example, this will yield one set of experiences – lateral views of the iguana moving from Shadow's left to Shadow's right. If he is standing to the west, the iguana's movement would be from right to left. If Shadow is standing to the south, the resulting experiences will be quite different: they will be experiences of a tail and haunches – if iguanas have haunches – moving away from Shadow. They will be different again if Shadow is already to the north of the iguana – in which case, an iguana's face will grow larger as it moves towards Shadow. In this sense, Shadow is implicated in the predictions he makes about the relationships between contingencies and consequences. He is part of those predictions; he tacitly features in them. And it is these predictions that allow him to see. There is a kind of – implicit, tacit – awareness of self that is built into the process of seeing. This kind of awareness is what, terminologically inspired by Sartre, I have called 'pre-reflection' – a contraction of his expression, 'pre-reflective self-awareness'.

The predictive nature of vision means that a form of self-awareness is built into any visual experience. This is for the simple reason that such awareness is implicit in the predictions that allow one to see. To be visually aware of the world is, at the same time, to be aware of yourself. This is, I should emphasize, not self-awareness in the sense of reflection. When you are getting on with the simple business of seeing things, you do not constantly think thoughts about yourself ('If I move there, the chaseable thing will do this', etc.). That would be far too distracting, among other things. Rather, the kind of self-awareness bound up in vision is pre-reflection, a form of implicit self-awareness that is part and parcel of any visual experience. Any creature that has conscious visual experience will be pre-reflectively aware of itself. Dogs clearly have visual experience, and vision is widely distributed through the animal world. We should conclude that dogs, and many, many other animals, are aware of themselves in at least the pre-reflective sense. You don't need to pass the mirror test to be capable of this kind of awareness. Mirror self-recognition does not test for this form of self-awareness, and neither do its olfactory variants. Regardless of his success rate on these tests, Shadow is as capable of pre-reflection as I am.

Self-awareness, then, comes in at least two varieties. There is the explicit, reflective self-awareness that is tested for in the mirror self-recognition test (and in olfactory variants of that test). This I have called *reflection*. Reflection – reflective self-awareness – allows one to think thoughts about oneself and one's body, about what one is thinking and about what one is doing. Then there is implicit, pre-reflective self-awareness – *pre-reflection* – that is inextricably a part of having conscious visual experiences. Anything that sees the world will be pre-reflectively aware of itself, and dogs certainly fall into this category. But only creatures capable of thinking about themselves and what they are doing will be *reflectively* self-aware.

The category of reflection, however, is not a simple one. The idea of thinking about oneself and what one is doing covers at least two different things. You can think about your body – the kind of thinking you might do when looking in a mirror. 'Yup, that's me', 'Could do with losing a few pounds', and so on. But you can also think about what is going on in your mind, about what you are thinking, feeling, about your hopes, fears, aspirations and the like. This ability is very different from that of bodily self-identification. It is a meta-cognitive ability – an ability to cognize about cognition, broadly understood. Awareness of one's body and awareness of one's mind are two very different abilities. There is nothing in mirror self-recognition that demonstrates an ability to engage in the second – meta-cognitive – form of reflection. The mirror test simply does not test for this latter kind of reflection.

Can dogs engage in reflection in this meta-cognitive sense? Most philosophers think it is unlikely. To think about one of your thoughts, you would have to understand what a thought is, and it's not clear, to most philosophers at least, how a dog would acquire the ability to do that. The most widely accepted account today is that the ability to think about your own mind piggybacks on the ability to think about the minds of others. You first learn to understand what it is for someone else to think something, or to want something, and then you learn to apply the concepts of thinking and wanting to yourself. The ability to understand the minds of others is sometimes known as a *theory of mind*. So the current orthodoxy is, in effect, that meta-cognition is grounded in, and built on, a theory of mind.

Given this assumption, quite a bit of research was conducted with a view to establishing whether animals (for the most part, great apes) can take another's perspective (specifically a visual perspective). To test this, in a now-classic study, Brian Hare, Josep Call and Michael Tomasello arranged for two chimpanzees – one dominant, the other subordinate – to take part in an experiment that tested whether one chimpanzee could understand the visual perspective of another – and so, in effect, know what the other chimp knows. Chimpanzees are well known to be rather irascible, pugilistic creatures, and one thing you don't want to do if you are a subordinate chimp is annoy a dominant counterpart – for example, by trying to take a bit of food he had his eye on. With this in mind, the two chimps were placed behind doors at opposite ends of an enclosure. The experimenter placed food in the enclosure under various conditions of visibility. Sometimes the dominant chimp could see the food being placed and sometimes he couldn't (in the latter case, an opaque barrier was placed in the door in front of him). The subordinate chimp could always see the food being placed, and sometimes was able to see whether the dominant chimp could see the food being placed (that is, the subordinate chimp could sometimes see whether the opaque barrier had been placed in front of his dominant competitor). The chimps were then allowed to enter the enclosure. The results: the subordinate chimp retrieved a significantly larger percentage of food when it was in a position to know that the dominant chimp could not see the food being placed.

One interpretation of these results is that the

subordinate chimp understood the visual perspective of the dominant chimp. That is, it understood what the dominant chimp could see and what it couldn't. If that was indeed the case, it understood the concept of seeing, which would be a rudimentary example of theory of mind. There are, however, other competing – and deflationary – interpretations. Perhaps the subordinate chimp was merely operating with a series of behavioural rules of thumb such as: if the dominant chimp is orientated towards the food – that is, facing it with no obstacles in between – then it will probably go for the food (and I, therefore, should not). I am not convinced of the plausibility of this kind of deflationary interpretation, but will leave it there – for this is, after all, a book about dogs and not chimpanzees. Even if chimpanzees do have a rudimentary theory of mind, based on an understanding of the concept of seeing and, perhaps, knowing, this does not mean that they understand other mental states: thoughts, feelings, beliefs, desires, hopes, fears, expectations and so on. A rudimentary theory of mind is one thing, but a comprehensive theory is quite another. And even if they did have a comprehensive theory of mind, this doesn't mean that they have taken the extra step of translating this theory into meta-cognitive abilities – that is, that they are able to apply this theory to their own minds. This is where we are with chimpanzees at present. The evidence for meta-cognition in dogs is even sparser.

Self-awareness comes in three different forms. There is the basic distinction between pre-reflection and reflection. But the category of reflection breaks down into two. First, there is bodily self-identification, broadly understood as the ability to think about one's body (and what is going in it). Second, there is meta-cognition, broadly understood as the ability to think about one's mind and what is going on in it. We can, cautiously, draw some conclusions about the extent of self-awareness in dogs. This is the current state of play in what we think we know about these matters:

	Pre-reflection	Reflection (bodily self-identification)	Reflection (meta-cognition)
Humans	Yes	Yes	Yes
Dogs	Yes	Maybe	No

Humans, at least when they get to around three to four years of age, are capable of self-awareness of all three kinds – pre-reflection and both forms of reflection. Dogs are clearly capable of pre-reflection, as this is part and parcel of having even basic conscious experiences. If dogs are conscious at all, they are thereby pre-reflectively aware of themselves. Dogs may also be aware of themselves reflectively – in the first sense of reflection. I think the jury is still very much out on this question. Much depends on how we interpret mirror self-recognition tests and olfactory variations on them, but there is nothing there that allows us to conclude anything with much confidence. With the second form of reflection – meta-cognition – we may be able to draw firmer conclusions: there is no evidence of dogs having meta-cognitive abilities.

One thing you can say about nature is that it tends to not have too much time for dichotomies, preferring instead the rolling landscapes of distinctions, graded to a greater or lesser degree. There are exceptions of course, but the issue of self-awareness provides a good example of this general predilection. If we start off with a dichotomous question – are dogs self-aware or are they not? – then this is quickly replaced by a more gradualist successor because, as we have already seen, there are at least three different types of self-awareness (one version is pre-reflective, the other two versions are reflective). The real question, accordingly, becomes: in what sense, and to what extent, are dogs self-aware?

Nature may not be fond of dichotomies, but we humans certainly are. This is because they serve a purpose that we hold very dear: they enable us to differentiate ourselves from, and more importantly (in our eyes), elevate ourselves above, the rest of the natural world. Of course, if we had been more observant creatures, we might have realized that our obsessive need to differentiate ourselves from other animals was the thing that differentiated ourselves from other animals. No other animal cares about that! But we didn't seem to notice this, perhaps because this drive to differentiate ourselves was insufficiently elevating. Because of these basic human proclivities, when we are faced with more than one variety of what we thought was the same thing, there is a question that we humans often find irresistible: *which one is better?* We like this sort of question. Moreover, when answering this question, we are just as often guided by a singular consideration: *which one is more human?* The more human a quality, the better – or so we humans tend to think.

For us, therefore, the years immediately following the mirror test's inception must have been quite heady. History hadn't been kind to our previous proposals regarding what differentiated ourselves from other animals – rationality, language, tool use, play, etc. It turns out that animals could be and do these other things too. But with mirror self-recognition, and the capacity for reflection it reveals, perhaps, we thought, we had finally found it. Reflection, the ability to think thoughts about oneself: what a wonderful, and uniquely human, ability! To the extent humans recognized pre-reflection at all – and those unversed in certain relevant philosophical traditions were largely unaware of it – they could regard it as common as muck. Any conscious creature will have that. But reflection, that is just so human; so remarkably *elevating*!

Unfortunately for our human vanity, the failure of other animals to pass the mirror test was largely an artefact of a failure to test them. When we finally got around to doing so, the list of reflectively self-aware animals began to expand inexorably. Chimpanzees, bonobos and orangutans: they are the animals most like us, that's why they pass the test. Reflection, then: restricted to humans and the animals most like humans. Then, however, dolphins displayed a distinct aptitude for the test. Okay, we humans said: they're quite smart too – the most intelligent marine creature, after all. Reflection became understood as a mark of intelligence – of which humans had the most, of course. Elephants? They do have big brains, of course. By the time pigeons got in on the act, human patience was wearing thin. Those psittacotic little bastards! But it was fish – manta rays and even the humble wrasse – that really rubbed human noses in it when they seemingly displayed a facility for the test too.

We needn't have worried. There are rarely hard boundaries in nature, life preferring, as I mentioned above, degrees rather than dichotomies. Even if other animals can think about themselves, it is clear that humans are much better at this than any other species. Practice makes perfect, and humans think about themselves all the time. Entire lives can be spent in reflective purgatory. We have taken this ability for reflection – an ability that at least a few species have in a basic form – and made it our own. No longer a basic form, but an art form. Libraries could be filled with books that comprise nothing more than page after page of tortured self-analysis. Have you read Proust? Or Rilke? Entire branches of academic disciplines have been invented to study reflection. Wilhelm Wundt? Sigmund Freud? In this muddied world, very few truths are as clear as this one: even if other animals can do it to some extent, humans are the world heavyweight champions of thinking about themselves. Reflection is, for all intents and purposes, ours. We have made it so.

🐾

The general human consensus is that reflection is a good thing. But the development of any capacity, whether biological or cultural, is not often an unqualified success, with no deficits or costs whatsoever. It's always a matter of swings and roundabouts. Remember the sea squirt's attitude towards brains? Remember what the development of writing did to natural, biological memory? Any capacity, especially when it is excessively exercised, will have its costs as well as its benefits, and reflection is no exception.

The cost of reflection is not unduly difficult to discern. Reflection splits you in two. Whenever you recognize yourself in the mirror, there is now more than one you. There is the you that recognizes and the you that is recognized. Whenever you think about yourself, there are two versions of you. The you that thinks and the you that is thought about. Reflection bifurcates — dividing the reflective creature into the one that is reflecting and the one that is reflected upon. Dividing each one of us into an actor and a spectator. The actor lives. The spectator watches. More than watches, the spectator scrutinizes. The spectator evaluates and judges. Split in two, we can never again be whole — single, undivided, of one heart and one mind. Thus, we live, and at the same time we watch ourselves doing this. We can never be fully immersed in our lives; never be quite fully committed to what we think and do. Not committed in the way a dog can be committed to the pursuit of iguanas on the stormy banks of a Miami canal. Whenever we are committed to something, there is a part of us that watches – that scrutinizes, evaluates and judges this commitment. We can be partially committed, of course, and we may mistake this for the full-blooded real thing. But the division in us ensures that full commitment escapes us. Our commitment is always conditional. It is what we might call *troubled* commitment. For we are troubled creatures.

Suppose I have a belief. I am not thinking of anything complicated. A straightforward, uncomplicated belief. A belief I might share with Shadow. I believe there is an iguana on the ground in front of me. Part of me lives this belief in the sense that I act on it – not sharing Shadow's peculiarities, I might walk around it – and my commitment to it is shown through my action. But there is another part of me that can be (reflectively) aware of this belief – and so can assess it, critically scrutinize it with my beady little mind's eye. Because of this, my commitment to this belief is always conditional. It is conditional in a precise sense that is unique to creatures capable of reflection. It is conditional in that my continued commitment to it depends on the deliverances of my scrutiny, on the results of my assessment.

For a creature such as Shadow with a truncated

capacity for reflection, a belief is simply a belief. Shadow has his beliefs, and he acts on them when circumstances allow or dictate. Shadow believes there is an iguana in front of him. Perhaps there is. Or perhaps it is merely some tree debris. Either way, Shadow has the belief, and his commitment to the belief is exhibited in his action – in the slow, patient stalk followed by the explosive burst. If his contingency–consequence predictions turn out to be unfulfilled – if the supposed iguana does not break for the water, for example – he will no doubt come to revise this belief. But while he has it, he is comfortable with it. He does not question it, and his commitment to it is beyond doubt. The belief will be abandoned only if the world does not play ball.

For a creature who is not self-aware, a belief is simply a belief. One has it or one does not. Once awareness of the belief – a complicated form of self-awareness – enters the picture, everything changes. Simple, unstinting commitment to a belief is no longer possible. Precisely because the believer is aware of the belief, she stands apart from it. The belief can no longer command automatic assent. Crucially, it can be rejected independently of anything the world does or does not do. Shadow might reject the belief that there is an iguana in front of him when it does not make a break for the safety of the canal – when the world does not play ball. Any creature that could not revise its beliefs in the face of an uncooperative world – a world that does not echo these beliefs – would not last long. However, until the world fails to cooperate – until it declines to satisfy his predictions – Shadow's commitment to his belief is unquestioned.

Our commitment, however, is never similarly absolute. We can revise, reject or abandon our beliefs independently of anything the world does or does not do. We don't need the world to adjudicate our beliefs. We can do that ourselves. Our beliefs can die at our own hands rather than at the hands of the world. Reflection gives us the ability to murder our own beliefs. It means our beliefs are always in jeopardy – they stand in peril of a critical scrutiny that is made possible by reflection. The spectre of doubt has come to haunt all our beliefs, and it is our capacity for reflection that has summoned this spectre. Of course, there may be many beliefs that a human never comes to reject. But it is not the actuality of rejection that is germane but its possibility. The possibility of rejection is always there, quite independently of what transpires in the world. For a reflective creature, this possibility can never be rescinded. Our belief is, as Sartre once observed, always now troubled belief.

The same is true of any other mental state of which one is reflectively aware. In these, the spectre of rejection perpetually haunts us too. I cherish a hope, perhaps. But is this really a hope I dare hope? Is it a hope in which I should invest myself? I have a desire. I know I have it. But should I? Should I not desire something else? Beliefs, desires, hopes, fears are the core of any human mental life. But once we are aware of this mental life, the real possibility of rejecting it, or parts of it, always presents itself, a rejection engineered by us rather than mandated by the world. Reflection is, therefore, the death of full-blooded commitment. Shadow's mind is serene: unruffled, untroubled, an early-morning sea on a summer's day. But the minds of creatures of reflection are choppy and never calm. They are the seas of the afternoon wind. Troubled waters. And a creature with a mind like this is, of course, a troubled creature. We are such creatures. Our capacity for reflection has made us so.

When self-awareness dawned, we became no longer simply the actors or authors of our lives – as Shadow is still the author of his – but also spectators of those lives. As spectators, we are no longer fully immersed in life – we also, to an extent, stand apart from it. We could no longer remain fully immersed. There is but a short distance to travel between spectator and judge. And as judges of ourselves, full, unquestioning commitment to our lives is now beyond us. This is the human predicament. Scepticism is our lot, commitment a dream of yesterday. It is no coincidence that ancient philosophy, the philosophy of Socrates and his students, was so obsessed with what it is possible for us to know. It is no coincidence that modern philosophy was born in doubt: the radical, methodological doubt of René Descartes. Doubt runs deep in us. It is our birthright and our heart-blood. Dogs are creatures of commitment. But humans are creatures of doubt.

Reflection has made us fractured, uneasy creatures, never quite at home in the world or even in our own skins. In his purest moments of pursuit, there is no gap between what Shadow does and what he is. That is a prelapsarian commitment that we can rarely, if ever, emulate. Shadow is the author of his life, and his actions stem from what he is: one heart and one mind undivided. We are the authors of our lives, but we are also spectators of them and, all too often, harping critics of them. Our minds are divided against themselves, as are our hearts. We are troubled creatures, existentially divided, riven by reflection. There is a hole in each of us, like a worm at the core of an apple.

4

A Gambler's Freedom

> Anguish in the face of the past ... is that of the gambler who has freely and sincerely decided not to gamble anymore and who, when he approaches the gaming table, suddenly sees all his resolutions melt away.
>
> —Jean-Paul Sartre, *Being and Nothingness*

Our exile from Eden set us free, but this was hardly a good thing. There was some small print we didn't notice. We had always been free in the manner of other creatures. Our fall, however, introduced us to a new form of freedom, a freedom that only creatures of reflection can have. Human freedom is very different from the freedom of dogs. For dogs, freedom is a field of barley, made golden in the sun. For humans, it is a glacial expanse, dark and nameless. In its coldness, its austerity, its monstrous dispassion, human freedom is almost ... inhuman.

In fields of barley, you will usually find rats. There are few things rats like to eat more than a good head

A Gambler's Freedom

of barley. The rats who have made their home in this particular field of barley are plagued daily by three monsters, all of whom, I am sure, would feature quite prominently in local rat folklore if rats had such a thing. The names of these monsters are Brenin, Nina and Tess, and they are creatures of the sky as much as of the land. They can smell the rats, of course, and probably hear their scurrying and rustling amid the sheaves. But they can't see them. To do this, they need elevation, a synoptic view. And so they leap, as high as they can, into the sky, backs arched like startled cats, legs pointed out beneath them as if they were being hoisted by an invisible crane, heads whipping around rapidly to survey the world beneath. In this endeavour, hang time is everything. If, from the heights, they spy a rat, they will land and then dart in its direction. But if they don't, that's when the show really begins. As they land in the barley, they disappear for a moment – the seas of barley run high at this time of year – only to reappear shooting skywards once again. And then, again, they leap, like furry salmon in a swaying sea of gold. Only rarely do these manoeuvres work, but they approach their task with an intensity and commitment that many years later, and many thousands of miles away, I will see echoed in Shadow's pursuit of iguanas on the bank of a Miami canal. In both we find the experience of freedom in an especially pure, quintessentially canine, and sadly (for us) nonhuman form. Freedom is different for dogs from how it is for us. How, you might wonder, do I know this, belonging, as

The Happiness of Dogs

I do, to only one of the species compared? The answer is that it must be different. This difference derives from differences in the structure of our respective consciousnesses, differences that only reflection can be responsible for. This difference is inevitable, as inevitable as the presence of rats in barley fields.

The seventeenth-century philosopher Baruch Spinoza was very fond of saying puzzling things about a range of topics, up to and including God ('a substance consisting of an infinity of attributes, of which each one expresses an eternal and infinite essence'). Here is his definition of freedom: 'that thing is said to be free which exists solely from the necessity of its own nature, and is determined to action by itself alone'. This is puzzling because the way most people think of freedom strongly opposes it to necessity. Necessity is all about the way things must be. But freedom, many people think, is all about chance, hazard, spontaneity – the way things might be, not the way they must be. Freedom is usually taken to be the opposite, the antithesis, of necessity. Nevertheless, I have come to think that Spinoza was right. It is just that the freedom he describes is not the freedom of humans but the freedom of dogs.

Any dog knows that if freedom is worth anything at all, it must be an expression of what you are. A free action is an expression of you. It originates in, and emanates from, your nature. As such it is not the opposite of necessity but its fulfilment. Freedom, in this canine sense, exists where nature and action align, where they are forged into a single *conatus*, a focused impulse, that then surges into the world. A dog's freedom exists where what it is and what it does coalesce into one indistinguishable expression of life. These three dogs leaping through summer seas of gold are freedom itself. I see the same purity of freedom twenty-five years later, in the moment I release Shadow from his leash on our first walk of the day, as he disappears into the sunny distance and lines of iguanas are sent plunging rhythmically into the canal. For a dog or any animal untainted by reflection, freedom is to act according to necessity, on the insistent commands of his nature. Shadow is at his most free as he scatters the iguanas to the winds. The iguanas are at their most free when they flee from his thundering advance into the welcoming water below.

Sometimes what is most important in philosophy is not an explicit claim, thesis or principle. It is the picture that underlies these things. What is most important about Spinoza's conception of freedom is the picture that we find beneath and behind it. What is your nature ultimately, if not your place in the world? Your nature picks out an identifiable portion of the universe and says: This is me. This is what I am. This is my place. This is my home. The resulting picture of freedom is, then, clear. Freedom results from your connection to the world. Freedom results from all the things that bind you to the world, pull you into the world, hold you tight in that world. Freedom is the world's embrace. This is the freedom of a dog. This is the freedom of belonging. For a dog, there is no other sort.

The Happiness of Dogs

Human freedom is very different from this Spinozist freedom of dogs. Our capacity for reflection has made it so. For a dog, freedom is an expression of nature. Freedom exists when nature and action are fashioned as one. But reflection split us into two, carved us neatly down the middle, and there was no longer a nature to meld with our action. Human freedom is a creature of exile rather than one of home. It is a creature not of place but of empty space. It is an expression not of connection to the world but of separation from it.

❧

Thinking of reading Jean-Paul Sartre's *Being and Nothingness*, but can't be bothered with the 800+ rather demanding pages? Here is a tip. Go to page eleven of Sartre's introduction, 'The Pursuit of Being', which is a synopsis of the book, that is written in harrowingly abstract terms. On this page, you will find two sentences which provide a very nice summary of the entire book. I get the distinct feeling that after these two sentences, everything else is, for Sartre, simply a mopping-up operation – a straightforward working out of their consequences. Here they are:

> All consciousness, as Husserl has shown, is consciousness of something. This means that there is no consciousness which is not a positing of a transcendent object, or if you prefer, that consciousness has no 'content'.

A Gambler's Freedom

There is nothing remarkable about the first sentence. It expresses a well-known view, associated with the phenomenological tradition in philosophy (and its founder Edmund Husserl), but also widely accepted outside of that tradition. By 'consciousness' Sartre means mental acts – acts such as thinking, believing, desiring, hoping, fearing, wishing, dreading, feeling, emoting and so on. That is, 'consciousness' as he uses the term means something like what we would today call the 'mental' – the collection of mental acts that make up our minds (although Sartre didn't believe in minds as such; as we shall see, for him, the mind was nothing more than a network of mental acts). Sartre's claim is that all mental acts are about something.

This certainly seems to be true of a lot of mental acts. You don't just think, you think something. That is, your thought is about something. You don't just believe, you believe something. You don't just want, you want something. Philosophers use the word *intentionality* to refer to the aboutness of mental acts. This term has its origins in medieval philosophy, and its use is a little unfortunate since today it has other connotations – such as doing something on purpose, or 'intentionally'. Here, however, intentionality doesn't mean that. It simply means aboutness. Sartre's claim, then, is that all mental acts are intentional in this sense. Their aboutness is what defines them – it's what makes mental acts mental. We can call this the *intentionality thesis*. Is this thesis true? It is obvious that many mental acts are intentional. But are all of them? Many people think so, including yours truly. But even if that turns out to be false, it is certainly true of many or most mental acts. There is, therefore, nothing unduly controversial about the first sentence. It doesn't strain credibility. If it is incorrect, then it is so within normal parameters. Nothing to see here, mate. Nothing new, at any rate.

This all changes when we get to the second sentence. In it, Sartre claims that consciousness has no 'content'. The notion of content he understands in a relatively straightforward way: a content is something contained in, or within, something else. Coffee, in this sense, is the content of my coffee mug. The contents of my pockets are a wallet, a mobile phone, and car and house keys. When Sartre claims that consciousness has no content, he means that there is nothing in consciousness. He means this quite literally. There is nothing in it. Unlike the first sentence, this claim is about as strange and radical as it gets. After all, if there is nothing in consciousness, where are we going to locate all the mental acts – thinking, desiring, wishing, hoping, fearing and the like – that Sartre has just claimed are all intentional? A bizarre claim, then, and most philosophers are not going to buy it.

Even stranger, however, Sartre seems to think that this claim that there is nothing in consciousness (a claim that hardly anyone accepts) is a straightforward implication of the intentionality thesis expressed in the first sentence (a claim that many people will accept and that almost everyone thinks is at least a serious contender for the truth). Indeed, so straightforward does he take this implication to be that he sees no need to provide any explanation or justification for his inferring the second sentence from the first. Sartre was a bit like that: *évidemment* was one of his favourite words.

One thing we can take away from the discussion so far is that it is often easier to read an 800-page book than to try to work out what someone was saying in that book from two conjoined sentences selected from the introduction. Easier but, I contend, nowhere near as much fun. And anyway, in the remaining 799+ pages, Sartre nowhere clarifies the point made in these two sentences. The other thing we can take away – and, again, this is me contending – is that Sartre was on to something.

To understand what Sartre is getting at, first let's get the picture right. A picture, in philosophy, is not so much an idea, thesis or view, but rather something that underlies these things, motivating them and drawing them together into a coherent unity. The picture that animates Sartre's remarks on consciousness is that of a hole. Consciousness is a hole in being – akin to a clearing in a forest (although the latter imagery is due to Heidegger, whom Sartre had read and by whom he was influenced). A clearing can only exist if there are trees around it. If there are not, then it wouldn't be a clearing but an expanse or an open plain. The existence of a particular clearing, therefore, presupposes the existence of trees that surround it and that are not part of the clearing. Holes are like that in general. They can only exist because of the non-holey bits around them, and so are defined by them. Holes are defined by their relation to the things they are not. Consciousness, for Sartre, exists as mental acts directed towards a world that is outside consciousness. It can only exist because of this world, and it exists only as a relation to this world: 'Consciousness,' as he puts it, 'is born *supported by* a being which is not itself.' It is merely a 'wind blowing towards the world'. Consciousness is a hole – a 'decompression' – in being. This is his view. Our unenviable task now is to work out why he held it.

The key to understanding Sartre's thinking lies in two ideas. The first is the one we have already encountered: all consciousness is intentional. Consciousness is always about something. This is the claim he makes in the first of the two sentences quoted earlier. Intentionality, or aboutness, Sartre thinks, is an essential feature of consciousness, and any conscious mental act, therefore, has it. Now, combine this idea with another: no object of consciousness is intentional. This is the bridge between the first sentence and the second. Together, these claims entail that no object of consciousness can ever be part of consciousness. An object of consciousness is something of which you are aware. So Sartre's claim is that nothing you are aware of can ever be conscious, or a part of consciousness. Consciousness is intentional, but everything you are aware of is not. Therefore, whatever you are aware of is, and must be, outside of consciousness – 'transcendent' was Sartre's preferred term. What about our mental acts – thinking, desiring, believing, hoping, fearing, expecting, emoting and so on? Are they conscious? Are they part of consciousness? As mental acts, his answer was: yes. Can we become aware of them? We can. However, when we are aware of these things, they cease to be conscious. They are no longer conscious acts. Indeed, for Sartre, who thought consciousness and the mental were essentially the same thing, they no longer qualified as mental acts.

As I have mentioned, the idea that consciousness is intentional is relatively orthodox. The crux of Sartre's argument will, then, depend on the second claim: that no object of consciousness is intentional. Sartre didn't have an argument for this claim. In fact, he didn't have an argument for any of this: in the last couple of pages, I have not been outlining what Sartre said but reconstructing what (I think) he must have been thinking. Continuing in that vein, here is what I think he is getting at.

We can be aware of different types of things. Most obviously, we can be aware of ordinary physical objects – tables, chairs, knives, forks, pepper pots and the like – and when we are aware of these sorts of things, Sartre's idea seems to be clearly true. These objects are not about anything. They don't mean anything. Of course, you can make them about something by supplying an interpretation. Planning a bank heist while sitting at your kitchen table, you explain things to your accomplices: 'Right, this toast rack is the bank. This cup of coffee is the armoured van. The pepper pot is the getaway car. You are going to drive along here...' In this scenario, the toast rack is about – in the sense that it stands in for, means or signifies – the bank. The cup of coffee is about – stands in for, means or signifies – an armoured van. The pepper pot is about – stands in for, means or signifies – the car, and so on. Of course, the toast rack doesn't really mean a bank, a cup does not really mean an armoured van. The meaning of these items is one added by you, the bank heist organizer. In essence, you have said: interpret these items in the following way. Whatever they are about, mean or signify is the result of your interpretation.

Sartre's insight – and it was an insight shared by the philosopher Ludwig Wittgenstein, who developed this idea independently at around the same time – was that essentially the same points apply whatever the objects of awareness. Take anything at all, it doesn't matter what it is, and if you are aware of it, then it does not have meaning on its own. If it means anything at all, this meaning must derive from your interpretation of it. This is all clearly true when we are talking about toast racks and cups and pepper pots. But let us consider some harder cases. These cases are harder because they involve candidates for things that might seem to have meaning on their own.

Sentences (and words, although some think a word has meaning only in the context of a sentence, and so I shall focus on sentences) are standard examples of things that have meaning. Moreover, we can be aware of sentences as they can be objects of our awareness. Let us all make ourselves aware of a sentence:

The quick brown fox jumps over the lazy dog.

There: one can hardly deny being aware of this sentence now. This sentence is certainly about something — a quick brown fox, a lazy dog, and what the former did to the latter. We are aware of the sentence, and the sentence is about, or means, something. This, then, might seem to be a counterexample to Sartre's claim that anything we are aware of has no meaning, aboutness or intentionality. This, however, is not so. In this case, just as much as in the case of the kitchen table/bank heist, the meaning of the sentence derives from our interpretation. The sentence is, ultimately, just a series of shapes against a contrastive background: lines, curves, loops, circles, etc. In themselves, these shapes mean nothing at all. They come to mean something only because we interpret them as meaning something. In this case, our interpretation is much more conventionalized than the one supplied by the aspiring bank robber. Our interpretation is mediated by the rules of our language that connect shapes with meanings. But it is, nevertheless, a collective interpretation on our part. On their own, these shapes mean nothing. We collectively supply the interpretation that imbues this collection of lines, curves, loops and circles with meaning. We supply the interpretation that makes these shapes about something.

Pictures might seem better candidates for things that might have meaning independently of the way we interpret them, especially realistic pictures such as photographs. With these at least, what they are about seems to be a matter of the way they look – and they can look a certain way independently of our interpretation – or so one might think. A picture of a dog, for example, is about a dog. And it's about a dog because it looks like a dog. And it looks like a dog independently of our interpretation of it. So photographs seem to provide a counterexample to Sartre's idea that anything which we are aware of has no meaning, aboutness or intentionality.

Once again, however, this appearance is misleading. Even in the case of realistic pictures, such as photographs, we cannot avoid the appeal to interpretation. Does a photograph of a dog look like a dog? To some extent, yes. But in some ways it does not. Dogs are not flat, smooth, two-dimensional creatures. If a picture looks like a dog, this is only because we have already chosen to ignore certain dissimilarities between the photograph and the dog. Thus, our interpretative work has already begun. It does not, however, stop there.

I have some photographs of my lifetime spent with dogs. Not as many as you might think, but some. So let's consider one of my favourites. There is a picture of Brenin and Nina running along Inchydoney Beach in Ireland. They are play-fighting, pretending to snap at each other, jaws ajar, teeth bared for the camera, as they run. What is this picture about? The picture could be about two dogs in particular – Brenin and Nina. Or it could be used as a representation of specific breeds – broadly northern breeds, malamute, wolf-hybrid, etc. in this case. (You know, the way a tabloid might include a stock photo of a pit bull or an XL bully when they don't have a photo of the actual dog responsible for an attack.) Or perhaps it could be taken as a representation of dogs in general? Or it might be intended as a representation of a mammal or of something that has fur. More abstractly, it might be taken as a representation of joy or happiness. Or, for someone who didn't understand the dramatic way in which these dogs played, it might be taken as a picture of savagery. Pictures, even realistic ones, do not mean anything – are not about anything – in themselves. Any picture might mean many things, and what it in fact means always depends on an interpretation supplied by the viewer.

Now we are coming close to the punchline of these difficult Sartrean ideas. It is difficult to exaggerate the importance of what I am about to say. Its consequences for human freedom are profound. It is a pivotal idea in *Being and Nothingness* – although Sartre never made this idea explicit – and so important do I think it is that, although I normally don't do this, I am going to italicize my summary of this punchline: *nothing essential changes if we make this picture a mental one*. Whether the picture is a physical one or a mental image formed in someone's mind, the necessity of interpretation remains. If we are aware of it, then whether it is a photograph or a mental image, we still need to interpret it if it is to have any meaning.

Suppose I form a mental image of Brenin and Nina running along the beach on Inchydoney Island – the same image as the one in the photograph. I can see this image 'in my mind', as we say. I am, therefore, aware of it. What does this image mean or signify? What is it about? Taken in itself, the same is as true of the mental image as it was of its physical counterpart. On its own, it could mean – be about – any number of things. A particular dog, a particular breed of dog, dogs in general, joy, savagery, etc. The reason it means something specific is down to my interpretation of it. In our mental lives the things we are aware of and our interpretation of them are usually bound tightly together as an apparently seamless whole. Typically, and certainly in this case, I don't first have a mental picture, wonder what it is about and then judge that it is about Brenin and Nina. The picture and its interpretation come together, at the same time. But while in practice they usually come together, they are conceptually distinguishable, as philosophers like to put it. Therefore, it is still true that if it were (somehow) taken on its own, the mental picture, as something I am aware of, could mean any number of things, and it means one thing rather than others only because of my interpretation of it.

Consciousness – in the form of mental acts of thinking, desiring, hoping, emoting, believing, wishing and so on – has intentionality in its own right. No one needs to interpret these acts for them to be about other things. Their intentionality is part of what they are. But objects of consciousness – things of which we are aware – are very different. Either they are about nothing or, if they are about something, their aboutness derives from an interpretation we supply them with. Acts of consciousness have what is sometimes called *original* intentionality. But if they have it at all, objects of consciousness have only *derived* intentionality – an aboutness that derives from our interpretation.

Since, according to Sartre, intentionality is the hallmark of the mental, and since no object of awareness has it, this means that no object of awareness is mental. The realm of the mental is restricted to acts of consciousness and never includes objects of consciousness. Some will think this is insane. Personally, I – perhaps of dubious sanity myself – think he is right. However, we don't need to follow Sartre all the way in this. For our purpose – that of understanding the difference between human and canine freedom, as experienced by respective members of each species – what we need to take away from this discussion are two claims, which we need to keep firmly in mind. Given how hard we had to work to identify these claims, and having recently broken my own taboo against italicizing, it seems I can't resist the urge to continue doing it. First: *nothing we are aware of means, signifies or is about anything on its own.* Second: *to mean, signify or be about something, any object of awareness must be interpreted by someone.* If you are still with me, many congratulations on getting this far! This stuff is really, really hard!

Reflection is the ability to think about yourself and about your body, but also about your mind. Through reflection, you can think about the things going on in your mind – your thoughts, feelings, beliefs, desires, hopes, fears and so on. There is a particular category of mental states that is especially relevant to the issue of human freedom. This is the category of states that cause us to act, and it includes motives, resolutions, decisions and choices. Through my capacity for reflection, any one of these may become an object of my awareness. And when it does, Sartre's general principle applies. As an object of my awareness, a motive, resolution, decision or choice has no meaning in itself. For it to have meaning, I must interpret it, and whatever meaning it then has will depend on precisely how I interpret it. This, according to Sartre, is why I am free. And this freedom is very different from the Spinozist freedom of dogs. In fact, whether this is a freedom worth having is a legitimate question.

Sartre is difficult to read – at least his philosophy writing is (his plays and novels are a different matter). But just when you think you are never going to have any idea what he is talking about, he steps in with a very useful example. Here is a typically helpful one. Our freedom, he writes, is the freedom of 'the gambler

A Gambler's Freedom

who has freely and sincerely decided not to gamble anymore and who, when he approaches the gaming table, suddenly sees all his resolutions melt away'. The gambler, we can assume, is aware of his resolution not to gamble. After all, he has carefully constructed and nurtured this resolution for quite some time – years, maybe decades, holding on to it sometimes, perhaps, with white knuckles and clenched teeth. It has hitherto reliably guided his behaviour, steering him away from temptation. But as he stands in front of the gaming table now and feels his resolution melt away, the gambler is faced with the unvarnished truth of human freedom. He understands that his resolution not to gamble is useless, and it is useless precisely because he is aware of it. This realization Sartre calls *anguish*.

Sartre explains: 'After having patiently built up barriers and walls, after enclosing myself in the magic circle of a resolution, I perceive with anguish that nothing prevents me from gambling.' The reason is that the gambler is aware of his resolution or motive. And this means that 'consciousness now has the task of conferring on the motive its meaning and importance'. As something of which he is aware, the gambler's resolution has no meaning in itself. Any meaning it contains must derive from the gambler's interpretation of it. Is this resolution a binding edict, one that brooks no exceptions, as obligatory today as it was yesterday? That would be one interpretation. Or is it, perhaps, the caprice of yesterday that can now be safely, and gladly, abandoned? That would be another. Two different interpretations, and there are many more available to the gambler should he look carefully enough. Each interpretation fixes the meaning of the resolution, and without some interpretation or other, it has no meaning.

There is one further condition that must be met for us to become properly acquainted with human freedom in all its wintry austerity. It is this: *nothing can compel any interpretation.* This follows from Sartre's general principles. If something were to compel the gambler to adopt one interpretation of his resolution over another, this would amount to a new motive – a motive for preferring one interpretation over another. But if the gambler were aware of this motive – and awareness of motives is what makes it a case of specifically human freedom as opposed to the Spinozist freedom of dogs – then the motive would thereby be impotent. The motive for preferring one interpretation over another would itself need an interpretation – which means we would need an interpretation of the motive for preferring one interpretation of the original motive over another. This leads to an infinite regress of interpretations, and there is no way of stopping this regress. It seems we are forced to accept this further condition: *nothing can compel one interpretation of a motive over another.* We are, therefore, free in the sense that nothing that we decide, nothing that we resolve to do, nothing that we choose can ever make us do a thing. The realization of this fact – the recognition of our freedom in this sense – is anguish.

A Gambler's Freedom

We are condemned to be free. The only thing we cannot choose is not to choose, for this is itself a choice. If you read books on Sartre, this is, depressingly, the usual explanation you will see of Sartre's view of freedom. It is an explanation that reduces him and his work to banality – a kind of *Reader's Digest* version of Sartre. Condemned we might well be, but not through our choices and not through the necessity of choosing. Choice does not arise for us. If Sartre is right, we are not the sorts of things that can choose. We are consciousnesses, and consciousness has no content. There is nothing in it to do the choosing. What Sartre is really talking about is not choice but absence of compulsion – not freedom but groundlessness. Our actions are not free, not in any sense of freedom we would recognize. Our actions are groundless. And there is nothing we can do to ground them.

This is the freedom of a man who sits in a restaurant, mulling over the menu. He is aware of the choices, but he cannot choose. The waiter has been sent away twice; more time needed, you see. But still no choice emerges. Eventually, when the waiter returns, the man simply blurts out one of the options, immediately wishing he had gone with something else. Perhaps he will amend his order. But that amendment would simply be another blurting out of an option, and he knows this too. We might call this freedom, I suppose. But it is a strange freedom. A better word is *groundlessness*. We realize, in anguish, the groundlessness of our existence. There are choices to be made but there is nothing – nothing we are, nothing we have done, nothing we have decided – that can compel one choice over another. No decision, resolution or motive – no matter how carefully we have cultivated and nurtured it – can ever make us do a damned thing. An interpretation of our decision, resolution or motive might do it. But the problem is there is nothing that can compel one interpretation over another. We always find ourselves back to square one. Choices to be made and nothing in us – nothing in our character or our history – that renders us capable of making them. In end, we simply act, and our acts are groundless.

The irony is, of course, that our entire lives are spend trying to build grounds for our actions. We are creatures of plans, of schemes and machinations. We are the creatures that, more than anything else, try to bring a future into being out of our present efforts. Much of our life, much more than that of any other animal, is designed to bring one future out of many possible futures into being. Or it is aimed at excluding certain futures and increasing the likelihood of others. That is what the treadmill of human life is all about. I go to school and work hard. My efforts get me into university, and I work hard there too. The result? I get to a better university. My efforts there get me a job, and then another job, and another, a foot up another rung each time. I write a book. Then I write another. All this endeavour – decades and decades of it stretching out behind me – done with the purpose of becoming a certain sort of person. A successful person. An admired person. An accomplished person. A person of means. Whatever.

Little did I know that nothing can compel me to continue along this path. Save in those rare but blinding moments of insight, moments when I realize – in anguish – the groundlessness of my life and of every choice and decision I have ever made, I continue down the same path. Until this path ends. This book is its own path. I write and I write, scrabbling away at my keyboard like a demented chicken, pecking, pecking away at the keys. I have resolved to finish it. Resolved, that is what I am. But my awareness of my resolution is its downfall. In my awareness of my resolve, I thereby cease to be resolved. The resolution means nothing. Any significance it has depends on my interpretation. A binding edict, or the caprice of yesterday? Nothing can compel an interpretation and my resolution is, therefore, impotent. I can walk away at any time. I come to the final full stop of the final page of the final chapter, and instead of one last peck, I can walk away. Like I did with my last book.

🐾

Don't worry. I did finish that other book in the end. And the remaining pages of this current book are not blank. Nothing is ever definitive with us humans, until our death makes it definitive. Even if you walk away, you can always walk right back again. What is strange about us is that despite their impotence, we generally adhere to our motives and resolutions anyway. Groundlessly free we might be, but you wouldn't know it by looking at us. There is a mechanism we use to combat the groundlessness of our existence and the anguished realization of this groundlessness. This is what Sartre called *bad faith*. Bad faith comes in different forms, but in the final analysis it is always a little story we tell ourselves about how we are not free. We are not free, the story we tell assures us, because of what we are.

I cannot walk away from this book. I am a writer, and accordingly I write. I am a professional, and accordingly I finish my books. This is what I do. I have children that need to be provided for, and so I work, I scribble, I expound. This is what a good father does, and I am, I tell myself, a good father. But as soon as I am aware of any of these facts about what I am, they cease to have power over me. In themselves, these descriptions and resolutions mean nothing. To mean something they must be interpreted, and there is nothing that can compel one interpretation over any other. I am beyond the authority of these resolutions precisely because I am aware of them. But, nevertheless, I tell myself a story about how they constrain me. A story about how strong they are and about how I am powerless to resist because of what I am. I am a good father. I am a writer. In doing this, I supply these motives with an interpretation. It's a sham. I can never simply be what I must continually choose to be. That I must continually choose to be a writer, or a good father, shows that I am not, really, either of these things.

A Gambler's Freedom

Again, it is the underlying picture that is important. Bad faith is an attempt to ground us. For anguish is, fundamentally, a phenomenon of groundlessness. I am groundless to the extent that nothing I am and nothing I have ever done can make me do a thing. What I am and what I have done provide motives for my actions, but I am beyond the authority of such motives. I placed myself beyond their authority when I became aware of them. My actions are, accordingly, groundless. To be groundless is to lack grounds, but what, precisely, is this? It is to lack foundation. It is to lack a firm, stable place to stand. It is to have no such place. It is, ultimately, to lack somewhere you can call home. It is to lack a place you can return to, a place where you can be safe, and where you know that everything is going to be all right.

Freedom in Spinoza's sense attaches those who have it to a world. As such, the freedom of dogs is an expression of home. It is an expression of the firm ground on which dogs stand. This is the ground of what they are. Human freedom, on the other hand, is a phenomenon not of home but of dislocation. It is a phenomenon born not of the world's embrace but of separation from this world. The freedom of a dog is an expression of what that dog is, of his place in the world, and of his place in his own history. But human freedom is always an expression of what we are not and can never be again. We are existentially deracinated creatures; our capacity for reflection has made us so. Human freedom is the freedom of exile.

5

Good Dogs

> Any animal whatever, endowed with well-marked social instincts, the parental and filial affections being here included, would inevitably acquire a moral sense or conscience, as soon as its intellectual powers had become as well, or nearly as well developed, as in man.
>
> —Charles Darwin, *The Descent of Man*

I became a father for the first time at the ripe old age of forty-four. Along with the typical worries of looming fatherhood, there were also some concerns specific to my circumstances. My new son would be sharing his home with two now-senescent canines: Nina and Tess. They had grown up to become very well-travelled dogs. To describe them as cosmopolitan would not be too much of a stretch. After Kinsale, they went on to split most of their adult lives between the UK and France. Then, following a well-beaten path, they retired to South Florida. The months of my impending fatherhood and the early months of my actual fatherhood coincided with their twilight years. Neither of them would see another summer. They had mellowed, certainly. But Nina could still summon something like her younger ferocity if she decided the occasion merited it – and passing dogs, mailpersons and cognate intruders, the usual suspects, all, in her eyes, merited it. And while Tess's predatory instincts were perhaps not as finely honed as they used to be, the squirrels of our new garden could attest that they had not disappeared entirely. Just the sort of instincts, I surmised, that might be triggered by a screeching infant. Therefore, I had my 'concerns' about how the new house-sharing arrangements were going to work out.

These concerns turned out to be entirely misplaced. Instead of bloodshed, I was regularly bewildered, and touched, by the tolerance and patience both Nina and Tess displayed towards this new pack member. Crawled on, dribbled on, kicked, kneed or gouged, they treated all these things with an unruffled fatalism. A finger in the eye or a tugging on the teeth were shrugged off with a Zen-like calm. Tess was calmer than Nina to be fair. In fact, she seemed to positively revel in it. But even Nina, old and crotchety, and despite the unremitting look of terror that animated her features, tolerated all of this with no official complaints. For me, this was a humbling experience: I couldn't shake the nagging suspicion that they were better parents than me. Certainly, their response times eclipsed mine. If my son so much as squeaked in the night, I would instantly find two cold noses pressed up against my face. *Get up and see to your son, you deadbeat dad.*

The experience was not only chastening but salutary. On the face of it – prima facie, as the philosopher in me insists on putting it – Nina and Tess were doing a pretty good impression of moral creatures, animals motivated by moral concerns. I would be hard pushed to explain their behaviour without invoking traits such as toleration and concern for another's well-being. When these traits are found in humans, we usually regard them as moral traits – as expressions of a morally good character. This moral interpretation of Nina and Tess's behaviour might have been completely wrong, but it did mean that, in those sleepless nights of early fatherhood, the germ of an idea was born in me. Perhaps dogs could be moral? Other animals too, of course. But dogs – two dogs in particular – were always my inspiration.

Even a cursory inspection of the media, social and professional, shows that Nina and Tess were not that unusual. Indeed, there are far more dramatic cases. Consider, for example, that of Khan (related in Belinda Recio's book, *When Animals Rescue*), a Doberman Pinscher rescue dog living with his new family – who, coincidentally, also had a new baby – in northern Australia. One day, not long after his adoption, Khan was playing in the garden with the family. He became agitated, pushing the baby with his nose. His agitation quickly increased, culminating with Khan grabbing the baby by the nappy and tossing him over his shoulder. The moment he did so, Khan was bitten by a king brown snake, the third most venomous snake in Australasia. Happily, and rather unexpectedly, Khan survived, probably because the snake had not injected much venom into his paw. The baby would almost certainly not have been so lucky.

Stories such as Khan's are not uncommon. This has recently become clear with the development of the single biggest repository of animal behaviour ever built. I speak of YouTube. Try it out. Type in 'Dog rescues dog'. But be warned, this can be addictive. But here is one of my favourite examples (even though it's immensely sad). On a busy four-lane highway in Chile vehicles surge past at dizzying speed. In one of the lanes lies a dog. Prone, unconscious, perhaps dead. Another dog appears at the edge of the frame and, at enormous risk to itself, weaves in and out of the onrushing traffic and — curiously, using his paws rather than his teeth — slowly drags the unconscious dog to the safety of the side of the road. In this harrowing scene the rescuing dog puts his or her own life in grave danger to save another.

In Khan and the unnamed dog of the Chilean highway, we find a kind of self-sacrificing behaviour of the proverbial throwing-oneself-on-a-grenade variety. When humans act in this way, we have no hesitation in describing their behaviour as morally good — indeed, morally exceptional. This category of moral behaviour is known as *supererogatory*. So morally demanding is this type of behaviour that we don't blame someone for failing to do it. However, precisely because it is so demanding, it is regarded as among the very best of all moral behaviours. Sacrificing yourself, or putting yourself in significant danger, to save another is one of most morally commendable things you can do. But if an action is morally good – indeed, morally exceptional – when done by a human, why should it not also be good if done by a dog?

Consider another type of case, less fraught but incredibly touching. Abandoned as a puppy at a junkyard in São Carlos, Brazil, Lilica was taken in by the owner and made the place her home. A couple of miles down the road, Lilica discovered a woman who regularly fed strays, and the dog travelled to her house every night to be fed. After a while, Lilica began to take a bag of food back to the junkyard where, incredibly, she gave it to the other animals who also lived there – another dog, some cats, a mule and several chickens. According to some reports, she initially did this to feed her puppies, but then the circle of her concern expanded. Whatever the reason behind it, Lilica did this every night, making a round trip of four miles on an unlit road. This behaviour clearly did not benefit Lilica. On the contrary, it took time and energy, and, the road being dark, involved a certain amount of danger. This self-sacrificing behaviour that is aimed at augmenting the welfare of others certainly seems to be a strong candidate for moral behaviour.

Even if they were familiar with these cases – which, by and large, they are most likely not – most philosophers would remain unconvinced by Nina, Tess, Khan, Lilica and the dog with no name. The behaviour of these dogs, they would contend, may seem moral – at least to the untutored – but it is not genuinely moral behaviour. For genuine, bona fide moral behaviour, they will insist, you need something more, something that only humans have. What is this something? It is our old friend *reflection*.

Reflection taints us in many ways. Some of these are obvious, but others less so. Existential dissection and the resulting anguish, uncertainty and inability to be whole are obvious consequences. A less obvious one is a failure of self-understanding. Reflection paints a picture of what we are and how we do the things we do. But it is an overcomplicated, needlessly convoluted picture. We are creatures prone to overcomplication, especially when it comes to ourselves. There is no clearer example of this than in our understanding of morality and what it is to be moral. Reflection dominates this understanding. In this context, reflection takes a specific form: the critical scrutiny of motivations.

In Chapter 4 of *The Descent of Man*, Charles Darwin provides an impressive list of examples of animals at least seeming to act morally. There is a baboon saving another member of its troop, a Newfoundland dog saving a drowning child, and so on. But just when you think he is about to conclude by endorsing the idea that animals can behave morally, he performs an abrupt *volte-face*: 'A moral being is one who is capable of reflecting on his past actions and their motives – of approving of some and disapproving of others; and the fact that man is the one being who certainly deserves this designation, is the greatest of all distinctions between him and the lower animals.' Animals, in Darwin's considered opinion, cannot act morally, because moral behaviour requires the ability to reflect on – to think about – one's actions and motives, and only humans can do this, or so Darwin believed.

In a similar vein, contemporary primatologist Frans de Waal takes seriously the idea that animals can act morally. But, like Darwin, he rejects the idea that animals can be fully moral in the way that humans are. Rather, he argues, they are capable of what he calls *proto morality*. They have the building blocks of morality – in the form of empathetic concern for others – but not morality in the full-blown human sense. His reasoning is very similar to Darwin's: 'Instead of merely ameliorating relations around us, as apes do, we have explicit teachings about the value of community and the precedence it takes, or ought to take, over individual interests. Humans go much further in all of this than the apes ... which is why we have moral systems and they do not.' We will only have 'explicit teachings', of course, if we can think about actions and our motivations – that is, if we are capable of reflection. Whereas Darwin's appeal to reflection was explicit, in de Waal it is implicit. But it is, nevertheless, there.

Neither Darwin nor de Waal pulled this commitment

to reflection out of thin air. Rather, they were, implicitly or explicitly, drawing on a couple of thousand years or so of philosophy which had arrived at the same conclusion. In the *Nicomachean Ethics*, Aristotle explains what he thinks is required for someone to act morally or, as he prefers to put it, *virtuously*. He claims that to act virtuously, first you must understand that what you plan to do is a virtuous course of action, and second, you must do it because you want to be virtuous. To act virtuously – morally in one sense of that word – you must be able to ask yourself: is this the right (i.e. the virtuous) thing to do? And if you decide that it is, you must do it because you want to do the right thing.

Aristotle was one of the two most influential moral philosophers ever. The other was Immanuel Kant, an eighteenth-century German philosopher who, despite profound disagreements with Aristotle on just about everything else, managed to end up with a picture of moral behaviour that was very similar to Aristotle's. Kant's view, like Aristotle's, emphasizes reflection. To act morally, we must be able to reflect on – think about or critically scrutinize – our motivations. In doing this, we work out whether these motivations are ones we should act on or whether they are ones we should resist. We work this out by bringing to bear on the motivation moral rules or principles we already accept. For example, Kant's preferred, and most fundamental, moral principle was what he called the categorical imperative: 'Act only according to that maxim by which you can at the same time will that it should become a

The Happiness of Dogs

universal law.' The basic idea is that if a motivation is a morally good one for you, then it must be a morally good one for everyone – a 'universal law' in Kant's sense. This translates into something very like the Golden Rule – it's a do-unto-others-as-you-would-wish-them-to-do-unto-you sort of thing.

The underlying picture, then, is: (1) take an inclination you have, then (2) reflect on it by applying your preferred moral principle or principles to it, and (3) identify whether these principles entail that you should act on the inclination or resist it. If you are of a Kantian persuasion, your preferred moral principle will be the categorical imperative. But there are alternatives. For example, the moral theory known as *utilitarianism* claims that an action is a morally good one if it increases the overall amount of happiness in the world, and a morally bad one if it decreases that level of happiness. If you are a utilitarian, this is the principle you would apply to your motivation: if I act on this inclination, will it increase or decrease the overall amount of happiness in the world? If you decide it would increase happiness, you should act on it. If you decide it would decrease happiness, you should resist it.

Whatever your preferred moral principle – there are many other alternatives I have not touched on here – the underlying picture of moral action is the same. To act morally, you must be able to reflect on – critically scrutinize – your motivations by evaluating them in the light of your preferred moral principles. It is very likely that neither Nina nor Tess could do this. *Here is a motivation I seem to have. Should I embrace it or resist it? Let me bring my preferred moral principle to bear ...* Nina and Tess had many fine qualities, but I doubt that the ability to reason in this way was among them. Therefore, in the traditional way of thinking about moral behaviour, neither Nina nor Tess could act morally. Sorry, girls. You couldn't have asked yourself a question such as, 'I am inclined to bite this annoying child who has grabbed my teeth. Should I embrace this inclination, or should I resist it?' Nor could you have brought your preferred moral principles to bear in attempting to answer this question. And since you could not have done this, your actions, while seemingly admirable, were not examples of genuinely moral behaviour. This is the traditional picture of moral behaviour. It has, among philosophers and scientists, been by far the dominant view from Aristotle onwards.

This exclusion of dogs from the possibility of moral behaviour assumes that the traditional picture is correct. And that, I think, is very unlikely. The traditional picture is, first and foremost, an account of what is involved in human moral behaviour – of what is required for humans to act morally. The exclusion of dogs and other animals is a consequence of this picture of moral behaviour being one that was developed specifically for the case of humans. And the first problem with the traditional picture is that it doesn't seem to accurately capture the way we humans act morally – at least most of the time. It is comparatively rare for us, when faced with a moral decision, to proceed by applying our preferred moral principles to our inclinations. Instead, we just get on with the business of acting well or badly. At a junction on US1, there is homeless person I often see. (At least, I assumed he was homeless – but the most recent thing he said to me was 'Dude, check out my music on Instagram.') He carries a sign, *'Ayude si puede'*. Help if you can. Sometimes I am moved by his plight and give him some money. Sometimes I don't. Either way, I can't recall ever applying my preferred moral principles to this situation. For a start, I am not even sure I have any preferred moral principles. But even if I did, my behaviour is likely to be driven by emotion rather than by reason, by compassion rather than by critical scrutiny. In this, I think I resemble Nina and Tess far more than I do the moral person depicted by Kant and Aristotle.

Defenders of the traditional model usually accept that critical scrutiny of motivations happens only rarely. Obvious truth sometimes has a way of compelling acceptance. However, they claim that what is crucial is that we *can* engage in this scrutiny. We can do it even if, most of the time, we don't. It is having the ability that is decisive rather than exercising it. This is a rather strange idea, and I can't help thinking it is a merely ad hoc – that is, unprincipled – stipulation designed to save a sinking theory. I can't think of any other case of this sort – where to do A you must be able to do B, but don't actually have to do B. To run (A), I need to be able to move my legs (B). But when running, I need to actually move them too. To play the piano (A), merely having the ability to move my fingers (B) would not be enough. I need to actually move them. In both cases, having the ability alone is not enough. I need to exercise it. It is difficult to see why having the ability to scrutinize one's inclinations would be essential to acting morally if you don't have to *actually* scrutinize them.

Anthropofabulation is a term coined by the philosopher Cameron Buckner. It doesn't roll easily off the tongue, but the idea it captures is a good one: a pronounced human tendency to provide overcomplicated accounts of how we manage to do things. Indeed, not only of how we manage to do things, but of how we must do things. Anthropofabulation, step one: take a phenomenon in which humans habitually engage. In this case, the phenomenon is moral behaviour. Step two: make up the most complicated and convoluted account of this phenomenon you possibly can. For example, when we act morally, we must critically scrutinize our motivations by bringing to bear on them our preferred moral principles. Step three: convince yourself that this is how you always engage with the phenomenon. Critical scrutiny of motivations via preferred moral principles: that is how we do it, that's how we engage in moral behaviour, all the time. Step four: elevate this into a necessity. Not only is this how we always do it, this is how it must be done. Anything that falls short of this overcomplicated standard does not qualify as an instance of the phenomenon in question. Only by subjecting our motives to critical scrutiny can our resulting behaviour qualify as moral.

In the case of moral behaviour, step three is already false. Critical scrutiny via the bringing to bear of preferred moral principles is not how we do it – act morally, that is – most of the time. And erecting on this falsity a subsequent necessity – this is how we *must* do it; this is the only way we *can* act morally – is merely compounding the implausibility. Most of the time that we act morally, we do not do it in this way at all. In fact, it is unlikely we engage in critical scrutiny of our motives in more than a tiny fraction of cases. Critical scrutiny of motivations, therefore, cannot be the only way of acting morally. The idea that critical scrutiny is what we must do in order to act morally, ironically, does not survive critical scrutiny.

🐾

There are even more serious objections facing the traditional reflective model of moral behaviour. Thus far, the problem has been that we don't seem to need to engage in reflection – critical scrutiny of motivations – in order to act morally. The next objection deepens this problem. Not only do we not need to scrutinize our motivations to act morally, but sometimes to do so can actually be a symptom of moral failure – more a sign that something has gone wrong, morally speaking, rather than gone right. There is at least one Australian who survived babyhood who is very grateful that Khan did not adopt the traditional reflective approach to being moral. If he had – 'I'm inclined to save this baby from the snake. Is this a motive I should embrace or resist? Now let me bring my preferred moral principles to bear . . .' – then the baby would have been dead before his ruminations were complete. Khan couldn't do this, I assume, but we humans can, and if we were to do it in this sort of pressing case, we would be morally culpable for our indecision.

It is not, however, just in time-sensitive cases that moral deliberation can be a sign of moral failure. Even if I have all the time in the world, critical scrutiny of motivations can sometimes be indicative of a certain kind of moral failure – one that the philosopher Bernard Williams has christened a *one-thought-too-many* failure. Suppose I know that in an hour's time someone will place a highly venomous fer-de-lance snake (known for their aggressiveness) next to two babies. There is nothing I can do to stop this (suppose, for the sake of argument, that I am currently restrained in some way), although I do have an hour to think about it. The snake and I are released simultaneously. Upon release, the snake will attack immediately. Having to act rapidly, I will only be able to save one of the babies. In the next hour, however, I will have plenty of time to plan – and justify – my course of action.

One baby is my son. The other I do not know.

The Happiness of Dogs

Naturally enough, I find myself inclined to save my son. Suppose, however, that, influenced by the traditional conception of moral behaviour, I insist on subjecting this inclination to a process of critical scrutiny. I might be a utilitarian, for example, for whom morality is all about increasing happiness or decreasing unhappiness. There is a detailed utilitarian story we might tell about my decision-making process. I am justified in saving my son, so this story goes, because failure to do so would cause more unhappiness than failure to save the other would. I would not only have the unhappiness that would accompany my son's death, I would also have the additional unhappiness that would go with knowing I could have saved him and so, in effect, am partly responsible for his death. The other's parent's happiness (for simplicity's sake, let's just suppose there are only two parents, one for each child) would balance out mine, but the additional unhappiness that would stem from my guilt would not be balanced out – and since that parent was not in a position to affect the outcome, their guilt would not be a factor. Therefore, on utilitarian grounds, I can legitimately save my son.

Williams argued, and I agree, that through the very act of introducing these sorts of calculations I am already guilty of a moral failing: that of bringing too much zeal to my commitment to impartiality. This commitment has its limits, and we breach those limits when we engage in excessive scrutiny of our motivations. I should save my son simply because he is my son. End of story – and a place where any moral theorizing would have to begin rather than a conclusion at which it might subsequently arrive. A dog would understand this very well.

🐾

Views do not become sacred-cow orthodoxies for no reason. People had their reasons for believing the traditional reflective – Aristotelian–Kantian – picture of moral behaviour. Ultimately, however, I think these reasons turned out to be bad ones. Specifically, they turned out to be confusions. Two of them did, to be precise. The first confusion is the idea that to behave morally, you need to have control over your motivations. The second is that critical scrutiny of your motivations can give you this control.

The first confusion is encapsulated in Kant's famous claim that, as he put it, *ought implies can*. By definition, a morally good motivation is one upon which you ought to act, and a morally bad motivation is one that you ought to resist. But to say that you morally ought to do something, Kant thought, makes no sense if you can't do it. Conversely, to say that you ought not do something, or you ought to resist it, makes no sense if you can't help yourself. Therefore, Kant reasoned, to act morally requires control over your motivations, and he believed that reflective critical scrutiny would give you this control. Dogs can't critically scrutinize their motivations, and therefore have no control over them. In Kant's view, their motivations do not count as moral ones.

Despite its near-universal acceptance among philosophers, Kant's claim that *ought implies can* is almost certainly false. I'd bet everything I own on this. The first thing to recognize is that there are several different kinds of 'oughts', the moral 'ought' being only one among them. And none of these other 'oughts' imply 'can'. There is, for example, the *prudential* ought, the ought of prudence. I ought to lose a few pounds. I really do. But there doesn't seem to be a damned thing I can do about it. Weakness of will, you see – *akrasia*, as Aristotle called it. Still, even if I can't – even if I am incapable of it – I really ought to lose a few pounds, prudentially speaking. Then there is the *logical* ought. If I believe that all bears from Minsk are brown and that Bruno is a bear from Minsk, then I should also believe that Bruno is brown. But perhaps I am so dim that I can't see this inference – 'How am I supposed to know what colour Bruno is? I've never seen him. I've never even been to Minsk.' If so, I have no control over whether I believe that Bruno is brown. But I still ought to believe it given that I believe all bears from Minsk are brown and Bruno is a bear from Minsk. The logical ought neither presupposes nor requires control. There is also what philosophers call an *epistemic* ought: the obligation to form your beliefs on the basis of evidence. Given all the evidence, I really ought to conclude that my wife is going to leave me. But I can't bring myself to do so. Just joking on that one by the way – to the best of my knowledge, an utterly counterfactual scenario. The epistemic ought – what you ought to believe based on the evidence presented to you – does not imply control either.

The lesson is that if none of these other types of 'ought' presuppose control, why should we expect the moral 'ought' to be any different? If anything, it seems, we should expect the moral ought to parallel these other types. This brings us to the next stage of the argument: diagnosing the confusion that led people to think the moral ought would be different. This is the diagnosis: Kant, and many others like him, confused two different issues. On the one hand, there is the issue of the moral evaluation of a person. This is the issue of how a person should be morally evaluated – as a good person, or as a bad person, or (most likely) as somewhere in between. On the other, there is the issue of the moral evaluation of a person's motives. This is the issue of whether his or her motives should be assessed as morally good ones, as bad ones or as neutral. These are different issues.

If a person has no control over his motives or resulting actions, then it is arguable that this person cannot be morally evaluated or judged. He is not, many think, a bad person if he did a bad thing over which he had no control. Neither is he a good person if he does good deeds that he can't help doing. If we are talking about the moral evaluation of a person, control may well be crucial. This, however, is not true when we are talking about the evaluation of a person's motives or actions – whether these motives or actions count as good or bad ones. Lack of control over one's motives does not disqualify those motives from counting as morally good or bad ones. When the moral status of motives is at issue rather than the moral status of the person who has them, a person's lack of control over them does not disqualify the motives from the possibility of moral evaluation.

Unfortunately, one of the most effective ways of illustrating this point is via the consideration of an exceptionally sad, immensely upsetting case. As a two-year-old child, Jamie Bulger was abducted, tortured and murdered by two boys, Jon Venables and Robert Thompson. At the time of this sickening murder, both Venables and Thompson were ten years old, and became the youngest convicted murderers in English history. Jamie suffered so many injuries that none could be definitively identified as the mortal one. Following the murder, Venables and Thompson placed his body on railway tracks in the hope that a train would make his death appear an accident. Under questioning, they revealed that they had planned to abduct and murder a child that day (and that their initial intention was to take him to a busy road and push him into oncoming traffic, though that aspect of the plan later changed).

Some theories of moral development suggest that Venables and Thompson were too young to be held morally responsible for their actions. I am not sure I believe this, and I am not asking you to believe it. Rather, I'm asking you to, for a moment, just suppose that it is true – a thought experiment. My point is that even if it were true, even if they had no control over their motivations, would we really want to deny that their motivations were morally bad ones? Such a denial would be the consequence of Kant's claim that ought implies can. If, according to Kant, you have no control over your motivations, then those motivations do not count as moral ones. They are neither good nor bad. This flies in the face of what I think is an obvious truth: the motivations of Venables and Thompson were morally horrendous, about as morally bad as it is possible to get. This is true even if they could not control themselves or their motivations. If they really had no control over what they did – I'll leave it up to you to decide whether that's true – then we might wish to refrain from morally judging them. But this does not alter the fact that their motivations were morally despicable, and we can still judge those. Whether Venables and Thompson were responsible for their actions is one thing. But whether their motivations were good or bad ones is quite another.

The first confusion, then, is the idea that moral behaviour requires control over one's motivations. There is no good reason for thinking this. Kant thought it – and convinced a lot of other people of the truth of it – because he confused the issue of the moral evaluation of motivations with that of the moral evaluation of people. To be a good or bad person, you might need control over your motivations. But for your motivations to count as good or bad requires no such control. The moral status of your motivations – whether they count as good, bad or indifferent – does not require you to have been able to control them.

🐾

Confusing the moral evaluation of a person with the moral evaluation of their motives was a serious error on Kant's part. Unfortunately, he then compounded this confusion with another. Having assumed that moral behaviour requires control over your motivations (which it doesn't), he then offered a spurious account of where this control over motivations came from – namely, reflection, in the form of critical scrutiny. When you (mentally) ask yourself questions such as, 'Is this a motivation I should endorse or reject, act upon or resist?' and bring your preferred moral principles to bear on this question, you thereby establish your control over this motivation. Or so Kant thought.

Having become acquainted with the arguments of Sartre in the previous chapter, we might view Kant's assumption that critical scrutiny supplies control as deeply questionable, perhaps even ironic. If Sartre is right, critical scrutiny of one's motivations does the opposite of supplying one with control over them. Becoming aware of one's motivations means that they no longer have any intrinsic meaning or intentionality. What they mean now depends on how we interpret them, and there is nothing that can compel us to interpret them in one way rather than another. Far from giving us control over our motivations, critical scrutiny only makes them groundless. You want control over your motivations? If Sartre is right, then the one thing you definitely should not do is critically scrutinize them, for that is likely to have the opposite effect.

Nevertheless, Sartre's view is controversial, and we don't need it in order to successfully refute Kant. When one goes about demolishing others' views, it is always best to do so while making as few controversial assumptions as possible. The problems with Kant's view are so obvious, you don't need to believe Sartre to see them. It is obvious that sometimes we can be motivated to reach certain conclusions rather than others. All of us, at some time or another, are guilty of ignoring certain pieces of evidence that are inconvenient for us, or our views, and of imbuing other pieces of evidence with an importance they do not merit. We all know this – entire political movements and systems have been built on this fact. Today, we live in a group-polarized world built precisely on the phenomenon of motivated reasoning – a phenomenon that sees many of us refusing to even access news platforms that might tell us something we don't want to believe.

In general, then, and as a consequence of this more global phenomenon, the scrutinizing of one's motivations may be self-serving. Indeed, it may be self-serving in a way that is beyond one's control. It doesn't matter whether this happens in your case, or in any particular case for that matter, it is the possibility of it happening that is revealing. The possibility on its own reveals something very important about critical scrutiny of motivations. Critical scrutiny of your motivations cannot give you control over those motivations unless you have control over your critical scrutiny. You have to be able to control your critical scrutiny – the way in which you scrutinize your motivations and the conclusions you reach from this scrutiny – if it is going to give you control over your motivations. But control was the very thing that was at issue in the first place. Therefore, contrary to what Kant thought, critical scrutiny does not explain control. The question of control that appears at the level of motivations reappears at the level of critical scrutiny of those motivations. This is another example of what philosophers call a regress problem. You postulate something (in this case, critical scrutiny) to account for a certain phenomenon (control over motivations) only for the same problem to crop up with your postulate too. Critical scrutiny, therefore, cannot explain control for the simple reason that it presupposes it.

It is likely, therefore, that Kant was wrong on both counts. The status of your motivations as morally good or bad does not require that you have control over them. And even if it did, critical scrutiny of your motivations would not give you this control. That concludes the negative part of my argument. According to (human) orthodoxy, only humans can act morally. I have tried to dismantle this orthodox view, showing that it rests on various implausible assumptions about the nature of moral behaviour – namely, that it requires control over motivations, that this control is supplied by a specific form of reflection known as critical scrutiny, and so on. If this negative case is successful – and I must admit, I am feeling unusually sanguine about its prospects – there is no good reason for thinking that animals cannot behave morally. From this we can now turn to a more positive project – that of identifying what moral behaviour in animals, and in dogs in particular – would look like.

The orthodox conception of moral behaviour – the conception associated with Aristotle, Kant and multitudes more – places critical scrutiny at the heart of moral behaviour. Critical scrutiny is one form that rationality takes – a form in which rationality is directed towards the contents of one's mind. There is, however, another way of thinking about morality, countercurrent certainly, but growing in popularity in recent years, that places emotion rather than rationality at the heart of morality. This alternative conception is strongly associated with the seventeenth-century Scottish philosopher David Hume. What we now call emotions, Hume tended to call 'sentiments', and so his view became known – perhaps unfortunately, given the current vernacular – as sentimentalism. When exploring the possibility of dogs acting morally, sentimentalism is a natural place to start.

Central to any sentimentalist account of moral

behaviour – whether in humans or dogs – will be the idea of empathy. Empathy is not a feeling but an ability – roughly, the ability to feel what is going on in the mind of another. It comes in two broad forms, *projective* and *receptive*. Projective empathy involves imaginatively putting yourself in the (figurative) shoes of another, imagining what they must be feeling and thinking in a particular situation. It is not clear whether dogs can do this, but it is probably unlikely. For them, the receptive form of empathy is likely to be more relevant. The best way of understanding receptive empathy is as a sophisticated form of what's called *emotional contagion*. The reason two cold noses were shoved in my face most nights, often several times most nights, was that the owners of those noses had detected distress in my son. His distress had infected them: his distress had, thereby, spread to them and become their distress. This is emotional contagion.

Emotional contagion is likely endemic in all or most social creatures. It is part of the glue that holds the social mammals and birds – and, indeed, perhaps iguanas too – together. I see it daily in the ducks and geese that frequent our canal as they collectively respond to Shadow's unwanted attentions – the panicked flapping of one quickly spreading to another, and another, until a mass take-off ensues. Iguana behaviour is often not very different – the panicked splash of one leading to that of another and another. This is emotional contagion, but a basic form, and not yet receptive empathy.

Receptive empathy is best understood as a

sophisticated form of emotional contagion. To understand the sophistication, it is vital to draw a distinction between two things that, for some reason, have not been distinguished in discussions of emotional contagion. The crucial distinction is between the cause of an emotion and what the emotion is about. Suppose my son's distress had simply caused Nina and Tess to become distressed. That is, they are distressed because he is distressed. This is how most people understand emotional contagion. However, emotional contagion in this sense does not add up to receptive empathy. The easiest way for Nina and Tess to alleviate their distress would be to go and find a quieter part of the house, where they could no longer hear my son, and get back to sleep. If they did, their distress would be over. But they didn't do this. Rather, their distress was accompanied by a desire to help – their primary focus seemed to be my son's distress rather than their own. This shows that they were not simply distressed *because* my son was distressed. They were distressed *that* my son was distressed.

The distinction between *because* and *that* is not merely a trifling distinction made by philosophers. It is the difference between what causes a mental state and what that mental state is about. If the dogs' distress were simply caused by my son's distress, then they could mitigate their distress by vacating the immediate area. But if they are distressed *that* my son is distressed, they can only mitigate their own distress by mitigating his. Moving to a quieter part of the house will not work because that won't alleviate my son's distress – and that is what their distress is all about. Their distress, therefore, motivates them to try to help him. Since they did not know how to do that themselves, they chose to enlist my help.

Receptive empathy, as I shall understand it, is emotional contagion where the other's emotion is not simply a cause of your emotion, it is also what your emotion is about. The distress of another, for example, is not simply the cause of your distress, it is what your distress is about: it is what philosophers call the *intentional object*, or the *content*, of your distress. When this occurs, an inclination to help is automatically triggered precisely because you are concerned with their distress rather than with your own.

That dogs exhibit receptive empathy – emotional contagion in which the other's distress is what their distress is about – can scarcely be doubted. A nice experimental confirmation of this sort of emotional contagion in dogs can be found in some unplanned intrusions into a series of autism studies conducted by Carolyn Zahn-Waxler and colleagues. Autism in one child of a family significantly raises the chances of a sibling being diagnosed with autism. Therefore, if you want to study the early development of autism and work out protocols for diagnosing autism in young children, hitherto undiagnosed siblings of children diagnosed with autism provide very good subjects. Zahn-Waxler devised a procedure for predicting the likelihood of a child developing autism. The procedure involved the mother or other caregiver pretending to have something in her eye, and exhibiting sounds and other symptoms of distress. The reactions of the children were then watched closely to see if they exhibited appropriate distress behaviour. Would they seek to comfort the mother, or ignore her? If the former, this was taken as a good indication that the child possessed the relevant empathic abilities and, therefore, would probably not go on to develop autism.

Interestingly, these experiments were sometimes interrupted by the family dog who, sensing distress in the caregiver, would rush in, seemingly to find out what was wrong and if there was anything it could do to help. In the children, such behaviour was taken to be the hallmark of empathy. It is difficult to see, therefore, why we should not also understand it in this way in dogs – in this particular case, after all, the dog was just an unofficial and uninvited experimental subject. Crucial to this qualifying as empathy is that the intruding dog engaged in helping behaviour. This additional desire to help alleviate another's distress is what elevates emotional contagion into receptive empathy proper, and it is best explained in terms of the idea that the dog was not distressed simply *because* of the mother's distress, it was distressed *that* the mother was distressed.

The neural basis for this type of emotional contagion is what is sometimes called a *shared representation system*. In humans, other apes and, very likely, dogs too, this system is underwritten by what are known as *mirror neurons*. The function of mirror neurons is precisely to mirror what is going on inside another. They do this by recruiting the same neural mechanisms in both self and other. Thus, if you witness another person undergoing (what you think is) a certain type of experience – for example, pain – then many of your neural systems engaged are ones that would be engaged if you were in pain yourself. Specifically, the same areas of the somatosensory cortex, the anterior insular cortex and the anterior cingulate cortex are engaged both when you feel pain and when you see another in pain. The result for the viewer of another person's pain is not exactly the same as it is for the person in pain, obviously. But it is something in the general vicinity of their pain: something unpleasant, aversive and pain-like. The existence of mirror neurons has not yet been decisively established in dogs. And part of me hopes it never will be, as doing so will require painfully invasive experiments on the brains of dogs. But their existence has been established in many other animals, including birds as well as mammals. The consensus is that, given mirror neurons' ancient evolutionary origin and their importance in communication, and dogs' impressive ability to communicate with us, it is very likely that dogs have mirror neurons too.

Those who sympathize with the idea that animals can act morally – we are a small but growing group, and we even have our own conferences – tend to focus on empathy and its products (such as sympathy, compassion, affection, etc.). I agree that this focus will be a crucial part of any case for moral behaviour in dogs and other animals. The advantage of this is that it allows us to draw on a robust and coherent sentimentalist tradition in moral philosophy, associated with the philosopher David Hume and the economist Adam Smith, that places empathy and compassion at the heart of morality. Any case for canine morality will likely be grounded in some form of sentimentalism, and empathy will be a central pillar of this morality.

Nevertheless, I think there is another pillar of canine morality that we cannot afford to overlook: inhibition. Empathy will only take you so far. How far will depend on the dog. For some – unusually saintly – dogs, empathy may be the alpha and omega of morality. I have in mind Marc Bekoff's dog, Jethro, of yellow-snow fame, discussed earlier. Judging by Marc's accounts, a more beatific dog could scarcely be imagined: Oh no, there is an injured bird! Don't worry, Jethro has picked it up gently in his mouth and taken it to Marc. If all dogs were like Jethro, we wouldn't have to look any further than empathy when working out the principles of canine morality. Not all dogs, however, are like Jethro. Shadow is not like Jethro. For Shadow, the trick is to get affection and inhibition to dovetail as neatly as possible. Sentiment is the foundation, certainly, but any gaps left in this foundation must be sealed with inhibition.

The Happiness of Dogs

The day after Shadow joined our family, he was playing with my sons in the back yard. They were young at the time, both under ten years old. He knocked one of them down and wouldn't let him get back up again. Every time he tried to get to his feet, Shadow pushed him back down. And every time he did this, his growling became louder, and his shoves harder. I could see the tell-tale signs of escalation and shut the situation down. Shadow tried to bite me as I did – but missed. Then, a few days later, there was his infamous first visit to my workplace, where he attacked my colleague's dog, and he did succeed in biting me that time. Three months old or so, and already with discernible red-zone leanings.

My plan for dealing with this was, in essence, to make Shadow addicted to affection. For eight months after his arrival, I slept with him downstairs on the sofa. Upstairs had carpets, which Shadow had identified as the closest thing in the house to grass, and this was playing havoc with his toilet training. So the tiled floors of downstairs it was for the both of us. Each night, when I began setting up the sofa for sleep, arranging blankets and pillows, he would jump up there and stretch, kneading the sofa with his toes like a cat. The sofa was L-shaped, and we slept head to head. I would often wake up in the morning with his paws touching my head. I have no way of comparing our Shadow with an alternative version of him, one not raised in this regime. But our Shadow became a very tactile dog who loved to be hugged. Indeed, little hugging can now occur in our family without Shadow, like an ignorant goat, butting in for his share. He became what some might call *soft*. To a degree, anyway – he was still homicidal around strangers. But with us, his family, affection become one of his primary values, something he prized above most other things. And around this value, it was possible to construct a kind of inhibition.

For Shadow, affection became what we might think of as a teaching value: a value that could be used to teach him. Since he prized it highly, affection became not only a way of showing Shadow that we valued him, but also a way of communicating to him what is valuable more generally. If one of my sons hurt himself, for example, he would be met with hugs and soothing words. This conveyed a message to Shadow: we value this one. If my son had been greeted with harsh words and a clip round the ear, a very different message would have been conveyed to Shadow, and his values would probably have been quite different. Affection towards others is a way of teaching a dog what he is supposed to value. But this works only because the dog has come to value affection himself. Through this protracted process, Shadow learned a value system. He was, in effect, inducted into our moral community: a community defined by, and organized around, value.

He still thinks about biting us from time to time. I say 'us', but it's really just me. Being the one who works him most, I am also the one who irks him most. A little while ago, I was doing some remedial leash work with him in preparation for our annual Christmas decampment to Universal Studios in Orlando. It was very gentle stuff, a watered-down version of the Koehler method. If Shadow pulled, I would stop abruptly (in the real Koehler method, rather than simply stopping, I would be required to turn and walk forcefully in the opposite direction). Yanked to a halt, Shadow turned around, snarling at me. I gave him a hard stare. He gave me a hard stare, then we returned to the business of walking somewhere. In moments such as these, but just in these moments, I think he really wants to bite me. His growl says, 'You're pushing it, old man!' My older son was present on one of these training episodes, and upon being halted, Shadow trotted over to him and mouthed his hand. Leashes are terrible sources of frustration.

That's the thing about morality. It always involves the possibility of inconvenience. Morality is a restriction one voluntarily places on one's behaviour in the quest for survival, and morality always has the potential to cost you. In morality, what you *don't* do – even though you really want to – can be as important as what you do. In this leash-work episode, we find a good example of the complex interplay between emotion and inhibition in the life of a rather complicated canine character. Leash work with Shadow is a crude behavioural modification that works only because of a value system that has been instilled in him from an early age. Without this value system, I suspect I would be toast. So there I stand, in front of a dog who, in these brief moments of rage, is contemplating biting me, but is – just about – prevented from doing so by his love.

Who is, morally speaking, the better dog? Is it a dog such as Jethro, in whom the milk of canine kindness flows freely, a dog for whom doing good or kind things seems to come as effortlessly as breathing? Or is it a dog such as Shadow, for whom doing the right thing is often a struggle, a fight against a nature driven by darker impulses? The corresponding question has been asked of humans and, after many long centuries of argument, no consensus has ever emerged. But we don't need to answer this question to discern the general contours of a canine morality. The morality of a dog rests on two pillars. One of these is empathy, the ability to take the distress of another and make it one's own. The other pillar is inhibition, the ability to make one's behaviour conform to one's values. We find both pillars in dogs. Empathy is primary. Inhibition occupies the interstices left by empathy, and only works if a foundation of empathy has already been established. What a dog lacks in one, it will have to make up for in the other. What strikes me most about this is how very human it all sounds.

Most of the time, we humans are moral in the way dogs are moral. There is very little in the way of critical scrutiny of our motivations in our moral behaviour.

Instead, our moral life is driven by emotions. These emotions are other-directed – aimed at the welfare of others, sometimes in positive ways, and sometimes in negative ones. The urge to help and the urge to hurt are both moral emotions. We act on these emotions, or we inhibit them, and out of these patterns of action and inhibition emerges the moral character of a person.

The reflective picture of morality – the picture of Aristotle and Kant, Darwin and de Waal, and almost everyone else besides – was an illusion. That is not how we are moral. Reflection on our motives couldn't give us what it was supposed to give us anyway. And yet we find it hard to shake this picture as an ideal. One might concede that we don't critically scrutinize our motivations very often, but nevertheless, we insist that we can do it and, when we do, we are being moral in the best way possible – the highest way, the finest way: the most human way. Only humans can be moral like this. Therefore, we are inclined to think, it is the best way of being moral.

I am not sure that this picture of moral behaviour is attractive, even as an ideal. To try to moderate our natural human biases, there is a figure I sometimes like to mentally conjure – that of the extraterrestrial anthropologist, an anthropologist from Mars, if you like. Imagine you are this anthropologist, sent to study the moral behaviour of various species on planet Earth. What would you find? What would your studies reveal? You would, perhaps, identify two different ways in which the creatures of Earth can be moral. One way, by far the most common, is that of other-directed emotions coupled with the ability to act on or inhibit one's actions. You also discover another way, far less common – indeed, vanishingly rare – that proceeds via critical scrutiny of motivations. A question occurs to you: is either of these better than the other? Is one of these ways of being moral superior to the other?

It is genuinely unclear how the extraterrestrial anthropologist could answer this question, largely because there are no obvious standards that could license this comparison. The question, the anthropologist might discern, is ill-formed; it is a question that it doesn't really make sense to ask – a pseudo-question. But perhaps the anthropologist has a preference anyway? Not a rational one, perhaps, but one based on the general 'feel' of each way of being moral. Morality based on critical scrutiny, the anthropologist notes, seems to be a morality based on doubt. That is not to say that everyone who is moral in this way must always be in a state of doubt. Rather, it means that a recognizable version of doubt is built into the model itself: I have a choice to make, the critical scrutinizer of motivations says to himself. What should I do? Let me examine my principles. Does this motivation that I seem to have conform to these principles or does it contradict them? Can I be sure of confirmation or contradiction? And how sure, for that matter, can I be of these principles themselves? None of this is redolent of conviction. This is a morality devised for a creature of a certain sort, a timid, indecisive creature, prone to the habitual second-guessing of itself. A dithering, faltering, neurotic creature. This is a morality devised for a creature of doubt rather than of conviction. Sometimes we are damned not by what we do but by what we think we should do. We are damned not by our actions but by our ideals.

A morality based on empathy and inhibition, on love and discipline, has a different feel to it. There is no dithering here. We love. We act. And we own both of these. This is not a morality for the faint-hearted. It is morality for a creature of conviction rather than of doubt. If human morality is more like canine morality than we often realize, if the morality of doubt is more the exception than the rule, even in us, this can only be a good thing. It is a good thing that we are often not the way reflection paints us to be. It is a good thing that most of the time, and in most of us as well as our dogs, morality is a visceral phenomenon, more a matter of emotion than of reason. It is a good thing that, no matter what our anthropofabulatory musings tell us, our morality is grounded in the two pillars of empathy and inhibition, of love and discipline. It is a good thing that dogs can be as moral as we can. And it is the best thing of all that, most of the time, they are moral in precisely the same way we are.

6

A Design for Life

> Operations of thought are like cavalry charges in a battle – they are strictly limited in number, they require fresh horses, and must only be made at decisive moments.
>
> —Alfred North Whitehead, *An Introduction to Mathematics*

It is time for an early-afternoon exploration of canine logic, its scope and its limits. As his daily life-affirming, meaning-imbuing pursuit of iguanas demonstrates, Shadow likes chasing things. All things being equal, he has a clear preference for animate things, but inanimate will suffice at a pinch. This early afternoon, midway between the morning and evening walks, his chaseable thing *de choix* is one of his many footballs (in both the European and the American sense – he has several of both varieties). To call it – indeed, to call any of his extensive collection – a football is to gesture to a past glory that no longer exists. He holds in his jaws a chewed-up, spat-out remnant of a football, a filthy,

The Happiness of Dogs

mutilated and decaying ex-football. The meaningful career of an average football will typically end in seconds under Shadow's tender ministrations. After its rapid puncture, it might take a few weeks to get the job fully completed. Eventually, he will strip it bare, skinning it like a carcass, leaving a rubber inner tube and very little else. But between its puncture and its ultimate dissolution, the ball remnant is still serviceable. Although no longer bounceable, it is nevertheless chaseable, and that is all Shadow has ever asked of a ball. However, his chasing of this cadaverous relic requires that I throw it for him. To throw it for him, I must first take it away from him. That is where our little afternoon dance usually begins.

Shadow drops the ball some ten to fifteen paces from me, and stands determinedly over it, head down. 'You know you have to bring it here,' I tell him. So he shovels it with his snout, moving it forward a few inches. 'You know that's not enough. C'mon. Bring it to me.' Another shovel with his nose. Minutes pass in this game of inches. This is a negotiation. There is a point at which I will decide he has done enough, figuratively meeting me halfway, and stoop to pick up the ball. We are just negotiating over where that point might be. If Shadow decides he has already done enough, he will start bouncing up and down, then feign a run from the ball as if I should already have sent it flying down to the end of the garden. I might demur: 'No, that's not far enough. C'mon. Bring it to me.' Or I might accept his terms. I stoop to pick up the ball. And then Shadow swoops in, grabs the ball in his teeth, and runs away before my ageing legs and back can get me down there.

Our negotiations have now entered a new phase. 'If *that's* what you are going to do, I am going in,' I say, and duly walk towards the door. Shadow picks up the ball and runs after me, prodding me with the soggy, muddy remnant. 'Well, you had better give it to me this time,' I tell him, and we begin our discussions anew. The ultimate result of these protracted negotiations is that eventually I get to throw what is left of a football for Shadow to chase. He brings it back – not to exactly where I am, but not far from where I am – and drops it in front of him, nose down, looking at me from under furrowed brow. You can probably guess what's going to happen next.

What is the most reasonable interpretation of this daily afternoon tableau? Shadow wants to chase the ball, and he unquestionably wants me to throw it for him. However, he wants this done in a certain, very specific way: without me taking the ball away from him first. Throw. But don't take. Don't take. Just throw. This seems to be a catastrophic failure of logic, and I tell him so. But Shadow, and dogs in general, have an unusual relationship with logic which, in the end, I can only describe as very smart. Even logical.

🐾

The ancient Stoic philosopher Chrysippus once told a story of a dog tracking a rabbit. Running nose to the ground, the dog arrives at a three-way branch in the road. He quickly sniffs the first two paths and, not finding the scent on either of these two, immediately runs down the third path, without bothering to sniff it first. Perhaps this story is apocryphal. But if it were true, it would provide evidence of the dog's ability to execute a logical inference of the following form: either A, B or C. Not A. Not B. Therefore, C. This is a three-option version of the logical inference known as *disjunctive syllogism* or, labelled in Latin for those who prefer their logical inferences old school, *modus ponendo tollens*. In its standard two-option form, the inference runs as follows:

Either A or B

Not A

Therefore, B

A dog that behaves in the way described by Chrysippus would be able to execute at least one type of logical inference, and therefore would be capable of logical reasoning. One of the most important things to understand about dogs is that they *can* reason logically. It is just that, all things being equal, and if they can possibly help it, they would rather not.

In recent years, a not inconsiderable amount of work has gone into trying to work out which animals can reason logically. Because it is relatively easy to test for, the ability to execute disjunctive syllogisms has been at the forefront of this work. There is a context to this, as there always is with humans. The context is provided by human beings' unstinting quest to feel good about themselves. As we have seen already, on more than one occasion, a clear human obsession – it's almost as old as human thought itself – is to find some feature that we have that decisively demarcates us from – and, most importantly, elevates us above – other animals. Historically, rationality has been one of our preferred suggestions for this demarcating, elevating feature. Plato claimed that humans alone have a rational soul. Aristotle concurred, arguing that animals have nutritive and locomotive souls – they eat, and they move – but only humans have, in addition, a rational soul. But it was probably René Descartes – the 'father of modern philosophy' – who gave this conceit its most famous expression: humans have a rational soul and by dint of this are immortal. Animals, on the other hand, are merely biological marionettes, not unlike the hydraulic figures in the royal gardens of Saint-Germain, very much in vogue during Descartes's life. A visitor steps on a particular tile and water is released into the figures of Neptune and a bathing Venus, with the result that the former advances at the visitor, brandishing his trident, and the latter attempts to cover herself. That, for Descartes, is what it is like to be a body without a soul. It is to be a purely mechanical being. Since only humans have souls, animals are purely biological mechanisms. There is no thought in them and no feeling. The lights may sometimes look like they're on, but there's no one home.

If humans were the only rational creatures – as Plato, Aristotle and Descartes would have us believe – then other animals should not be capable of executing a logical inference such as disjunctive syllogism. For if it were able to do so, an animal would show that it could reason in accordance with a law of logic. Unfortunately for these philosophers, several species of (non-human) animals have shown themselves capable of executing this inference. The experiments used to establish this ability are variations on a general theme. A test animal is presented with two opaque cups, A and B. Both cups are initially empty (and the animal is shown this). The animal then sees the experimenter baiting one of the cups, but precisely which one is hidden from the animal by an opaque barrier. The cups are then hermetically sealed with a transparent lid. Finally, the experimenter reveals that one cup – say, cup A – is empty. The animal is then allowed to choose between the two cups. If it is capable of executing disjunctive syllogism, it should choose cup B.

Animals that have passed this test include the usual suspects – animal luminaries such as great apes, monkeys and ravens. But dogs seem to pass it too, and dogs are by far the most interesting case because not only do they pass the test, they also show what I think is a healthy contempt for the abilities that allow them to do so. A dog will pass this test only if the cups are manipulated remotely and the human who is orchestrating the manipulation is hidden. If the experimenter is visible to the dog, then the dog will far prefer to use cues – and hence clues – gleaned from him or her. 'I don't know which cup it's in. Let me see if I can work it out from

A Design for Life

your face. You have these discernible tells, you know.' The conclusion seems inescapable. Dogs can reason logically, but they would rather not if they can get away with it. This seems sensible to me, and I say this as someone who has dedicated a lifetime to thinking. Thinking is hard! Why would you do it if you don't have to?

🐾

At least one other human with a lifetime of hard thinking behind him seems inclined to agree. In this passage, Alfred North Whitehead – the author of *Process and Reality*, and the man who described Western philosophy as a series of footnotes to Plato – nicely captures the canine attitude towards thinking (although he was talking not about dogs but about us):

> It is a profoundly erroneous truism, repeated by all copy-books and by eminent people when they are making speeches, that we should cultivate the habit of thinking of what we are doing. The precise opposite is the case. Civilization advances by extending the number of important operations which we can perform without thinking about them. Operations of thought are like cavalry charges in a battle – they are strictly limited in number, they require fresh horses, and must only be made at decisive moments.

Whitehead knew what he was talking about. In the monumental book *Principia Mathematica* – his

The Happiness of Dogs

collaboration with Bertrand Russell that attempted to derive mathematics from set theory – it took the first three hundred and seventy-nine pages to establish the 'occasionally useful' claim that 1+1=2. My point is that Whitehead spent much of his life thinking things that were hard to think. Russell once said that he believed his intellect would never recover from the strain of writing *Principia*, and that the concentration involved had 'actually damaged [his] brain'. It is difficult to imagine that Whitehead felt very differently. As a mathematician and philosopher, he was all too aware of the pitfalls of excessive reasoning. It seems, however, that this conclusion was one he arrived at through excessive reasoning.

Dogs, on the other hand, understand these pitfalls naturally; effortlessly, even. For dogs, thinking (e.g. executing a logical inference) is hard. But looking at a human face and working out what is going on in there, that's just automatic. All the time they have spent with us has given them the ability to read us with extraordinary proficiency. Dogs even exhibit what's known as *left gaze bias.* This is a tendency to focus on the right side of human faces because the right side of the human face, being controlled by the left side of the brain, more accurately expresses underlying emotions. Humans do this to each other, particularly when strangers meet, and dogs have learned to do the same thing. The extent to which this has a genetic basis is not clear, but one thing *is* clear: dogs find reading human faces much easier than executing disjunctive syllogisms. The latter, for a dog, is a last resort. When a dog faces

A Design for Life

a problem it cannot solve – or even a problem it could solve if it just thought about it for a while – looking at the face of its human is always its first port of call. The dog will do this automatically and unthinkingly. If Whitehead is correct, and civilization 'advances by extending the number of important operations which we can perform without thinking about them', this is a striking advance in dog civilization.

🐾

It is not entirely clear how long dogs have been with us. Current estimates vary from 18,000 to 36,000 years. Whichever figure turns out to be correct, it has been a long time. Dogs are the result of the domestication of the wolf, and it is likely that wolves domesticated themselves. Being palaeolithic killing machines, the newly burgeoning species of bipedal apes afforded many scavenging opportunities in and around these early humans' camps. Some of the scavenging wolves were better able to put up with the presence of humans – they had a higher flight threshold (reminiscent of Cocky, one of our Miami iguanas described earlier, who would always wait until the very last second to plunge into the safety of the canal). These human-tolerant wolves would be better scavengers, and this gave them a selective advantage in the struggle for life. This higher flight threshold turned out to have a genetic basis, and therefore the gene for toleration – for a higher flight threshold – was passed on at a differentially higher rate and became augmented over time, ultimately leading to the wolf's domestication. That this was an extraordinarily successful evolutionary strategy is a fact easily gleaned from the numbers. Today, there are estimated to be somewhere in the region of 900 million dogs living around the world at any given time, compared with between 200,000 and 250,000 wolves.

Some of the effects of this domestication are obvious: a general reduction in aggression and, accompanying this, what is known as *neoteny* – the development of characteristics that, in non-domesticated wolves, would be juvenile. In a classic study that began in the 1950s, geneticist Dmitri Belyaev began a breeding programme with silver foxes, reproducing from only the tamest, least aggressive ones. In less than ten generations, foxes were being born into his programme that were markedly different from the ones with which he began the programme. Belyaev wrote: 'Like dogs, these foxes seek contact with familiar persons, tend to get close to them, and lick their hands and faces.' This, however, was not all. These foxes exhibited physical as well as psychological changes – most notably, floppy ears (as well as, although the explanation of this is contested, piebald coats, a characteristic shared by dogs, cows, horses and other domesticated animals). Belyaev suggested, like Darwin before him, that there might be such a thing as domestication syndrome – a collection of physical traits that go with tameness.

Whether or not this is true, there is one feature of

A Design for Life

domestication that has generally been overlooked: a change not in physical or emotional traits, but in *cognition*. Through domestication, dogs found a way of offloading one of the most difficult and unpleasant aspects of life: *thinking*. Thinking is hard, and dogs don't like to do it if they don't have to. They can execute disjunctive syllogism if they absolutely must, but they would much rather not if they can get away with it. They arranged for us to do their thinking for them instead. In effect, we became part of the dog's *extended mind*.

🐾

Philosophers Andy Clark and David Chalmers once devised a nice little thought experiment that illustrates the general idea of the extended mind. They imagined the case of Otto, a man in the early stages of Alzheimer's disease. To deal with his memory loss, Otto writes down information in a notebook that he always carries with him. One day, he finds out that there is an exhibition on in the Museum of Modern Art and decides he would like to see it. He looks in his notebook and finds the sentence 'The Museum of Modern Art is on 53rd Street', and duly sets off there.

Clark and Chalmers argue, notoriously, that this sentence should be counted as one of Otto's beliefs. Their argument is that a belief is defined by what it does – that is, broadly speaking, by the role it plays in relating perception, desires and action. I see dark clouds gathering,

The Happiness of Dogs

and I desire to stay dry. I believe my umbrella is in the closet, and duly go and fetch it. My belief links my perception and my desire to action. That, in essence, is what a belief does, and a belief, for Clark and Chalmers, is defined by this role. But Otto's sentence 'The Museum of Modern Art is on 53rd Street' seems to function in the same kind of way. It links his perception (of, for example, the advertisement for the exhibition), his desire (to see the exhibition) and his action (going to 53rd Street). Therefore, they argue, we should accept that the sentence in Otto's book is one of his beliefs. The sentence is part of Otto's *extended mind*.

This idea is controversial, and I don't need anything as controversial for my purposes. All I need is the much more anodyne idea that external structures – like Otto's notebook, but many more things besides – can be important facilitators of our thinking, taking much of the burden of it from us. Think about the difference between doing long division in your head and doing it with a pen and paper. The pen and paper allow you to break down the overall process into a series of discrete, simple steps. Once you have completed a step, the results you have written on the paper will direct you to the next one. Much easier than doing it in your head. And even easier if you happen to have a calculator handy instead of mere pen and paper. In the pages to come, when I talk of the extended mind, all I will mean by this is the idea that external structures of certain sorts can be important facilitators of thinking and reasoning.

A Design for Life

In a classic study I mentioned earlier, Russian psychologists Alexander Luria and Lev Vygotsky examined the effect of the development of literacy on memory. Literacy is understood broadly, and includes early systems of information storage, such as the system of *kvinus*, or knots, employed in ancient Peru. Put yourself in the shoes of two different people. First, there is the tribal envoy of a pre-literate culture, tasked with remembering, word for word, the message of his tribal chief. Second, there is the Peruvian *kvinu* officer who uses a sequence of knots to record information his chief wishes him to convey. It is clear who has the more difficult job. All the *kvinu* officer has to remember is the 'code' – what the knots mean – that allows him to plug into the information contained in the knots. This code is, then, something that can be used for multiple messages in the future. The knots carry information, and as long as one remembers the code, one can readily access the information. The tribal envoy of the pre-literate culture has a more difficult task, as all he has to rely on in remembering his chief's message is his biological brain. But the *kvinu* officer has offloaded some of the difficulty of this task on to the world. He has more resources than his biological brain: he can rely on information contained in structures, ones he has created precisely for this purpose. The *kvinu* officer therefore needs to make less use of his biological brain as the work it formerly did has been taken up by these external information-bearing structures. The advent of pen and paper – allowing more efficient production and greater flexibility – would further augment the capacity of external information-bearing structures and systems. Today, of course, we keep this development going in the form of smartphones, laptops, desktops and supercomputers. The more sophisticated our external information-bearing structures become, the more possible it becomes for us to offload tasks on to the world around us. Sometimes the world may be doing practically all the work for us.

The impact of domestication on canine cognition is akin to the development of pen and paper on human cognition – and just as important for them as that development was for us. Humans are the external information-bearing structures that dogs like to use to solve the problems they encounter. It's much easier that way. A dog could execute disjunctive syllogism if he really wanted to, but why would he bother doing this when he has us around for this kind of thing? Think how hard it would be to divide 937 by 649 in your head. Pen and paper make this task much easier. The difference between a dog executing disjunctive syllogism himself and getting us to do it for him is analogous to the difference between doing long division in your head and doing it with pen and paper.

There is an old expression which, in the present context, is deeply ironic: why keep a dog if you are going to bark yourself? Barking is actually one of the few things we can't do for dogs. For most other things, dogs have taken this idea and run with it. Whatever they need done, they will generally find a way of getting us to do it for them. Imagine a slight variation on Clark and Chalmers's thought experiment in which Otto, instead of a book, has a human companion – I imagine this companion as a smaller version of Otto, a sort of mini-Otto, like Dr Evil's Mini-Me in the Austin Powers movies – who is always reliably there and can provide all the information Otto needs, whenever and wherever he needs it. 'You want to go to the Museum of Modern Art, Otto? It's on 53rd Street, mate.' To dogs, we are like this mini-Otto. Of course, this was never a fiendish plan on the part of dogs. It's just the way things turned out. For whatever reason, and by whatever route, we became their extended minds.

If Luria and Vygotsky are right, during the development of literacy in a society, the biological memory of its members tends to shrivel. Does this mean that our memory is now worse than in our pre-literate days? This conclusion, I think, would be incorrect. Our memory is not worse than that of our pre-literate forebears, but it is different. The incorporation of external, non-biological information-bearing structures into our thinking is a change in the *architecture* of our cognition.

Some people think our smartphones are making us more stupid. I doubt this is true; they may be making us ruder and more distracted, but not, I suspect, more stupid. I'm not sure anyone would want to claim that writing turned us into idiots, and smartphones are simply one of the most recent developments in a long history that began with writing – a history, that is, of our offloading cognitive tasks on to our environment. The locus of our intelligence has changed. Intelligence is no longer something located exclusively in our brains. It is, in part, located in our interaction with the world, and in what we do to and with that world.

Dogs' domestication – and their resulting reliance on, or exploitation of, humans – probably lies at the heart of their uneasy relationship with another kind of reasoning: *causal* or *mechanical* reasoning. Logical reasoning is reasoning in accordance with the rules of logic, and the execution of disjunctive syllogism would be one example of this. Causal reasoning, on the other hand, is based on an understanding of the properties of objects and how these may be realigned to further one's goals. Some birds, notably those of the corvid family, are notoriously good at this sort of thing. New Caledonian crows are arch tool makers, whittling sticks into hooks to extract food from hard-to-reach places, dropping pebbles into tubes to raise the water level to retrieve a peanut floating on top, combining different tools to achieve desired results. However, tool use in the animal kingdom extends far beyond corvids. Chimpanzees do it – using rocks to crack nuts, fashioning spears from sticks, and making pounding tools from parts of oil palm trees. Perhaps more surprisingly, tool use can be found in invertebrates such as octopuses – who fashion shelters from coconut shell halves.

A Design for Life

My favourite example, because it struck me as so unexpected, is that alligators have been observed placing twigs on their snouts to attract nesting birds. They only do this during the nesting season, apparently, which is, when you think about it, really rather clever.

Dogs, on the other hand, don't seem to be masterminds of causal reasoning. In part, this is no doubt because many cases of tool use – the standard bearer of causal reasoning as far as humans are concerned – involves having hands, or other things, such as beaks, that can stand in for hands. Nevertheless, even when compared with their wolf cousins – obviously also handless and beakless – dogs do not fare particularly well. This was highlighted in some well-known observations of wolves and dogs by Harry Frank as a psychology professor at the University of Michigan-Flint. Frank reported that one of his wolves learned to open the door from its kennels into the outside compound. To be opened, the handle of the door first had to be pushed towards the door and then rotated. Frank reported that a dog – a malamute – that also lived at the facility watched the wolves do this several times a day for six years and never learned how to do it himself. One of the facility's other inhabitants, a wolamute – a malamute–wolf mix – learned how to open the door after two weeks of observation. But a wolf then learned the task after watching the wolamute just once, and she used a different technique. The wolamute used his muzzle, but she used her paws. This showed that, rather than simply imitating the wolamute, the wolf understood the nature of the problem and what was required to solve it.

It's really no surprise that dogs should fare so poorly at causal-reasoning tasks compared with wolves. Dogs have had 18,000 to 36,000 years of getting us to do these tasks for them. One should, therefore, expect that their facility for causal reasoning would wither, just as the outstanding biological memories of members of pre-literate cultures withered in the face of the onslaught of literacy. Does this mean that dogs are less intelligent than wolves? No, it just means their intelligence is of a different sort. Memory didn't become worse in literate cultures, it just changed. No longer a purely biological phenomenon, in us it now straddles things going on in the brain and things we do to and with the world. The same is true of our cognition more generally. Cognizing – thinking, broadly construed – is something we do in the world as much as something we do in our head. The same is also true of our oldest companions. Reasoning, whether causal or logical, is something they get us to do for them. We are those things in the world in which their processes of reasoning are embodied.

In my view, dogs are a genius species. Who cares if they struggle with door handles? As far as a dog is concerned, why open doors yourself when you have got a human to do it for you? Their genius lies in making us their extended minds – not, as I say, as a fiendish plan, which would be beyond them anyway, but just a matter of how things turned out. Some might think this is lazy. I'm more inclined to the view that it is a very intelligent use of resources. We think we are smart because we think so much about everything all the time. Dogs think they are smart because they don't think about everything all the time – they keep someone else around to do that for them. Dogs are the world's great delegators, and their genius lies in a world-class knack of making sure we play along.

I used to think Shadow's seeming failure to grasp that I would have to take the ball from him before I could throw it was a catastrophic failure of reasoning – either logical or causal, or maybe both. But the scales have been lifted from my eyes. Shadow is simply delegating the details to me. 'Look, this is how I want it to go. I want you to throw the ball, but I don't want you to take it off me first. To be honest, I'm a little hazy on the details. As you know, details are not really my thing. You work it out for me, please.'

In this we find the perfect riposte to Plato, Aristotle and Descartes. For these exalted fathers of philosophy, ancient and modern, reason was the trait that demarcated us from, and elevated us above, the (other) animals. But Shadow has, I think, more accurately identified what reason is. Reason is just a tool, one among others in a largish toolbox, for getting what you want. It doesn't matter where your reason is located. You might find it in your brain. You might find it in the worldly manipulation of information-bearing structures. Or – and this will be particularly true if you are a dog – you might find it in the brains of others. What is important is not where it is, or even who has it, but that it is available to be used whenever and however you need it. Getting others to do your reasoning for you – to exercise rationality on your behalf – is, ultimately, a very rational thing to do.

One thing that most philosophers agree on is the necessity of having a rational plan for life. Maybe more than one such plan. The idea of a plan incorporates two elements. First, there is the idea of a goal: a desired future state. This desired state can involve you achieving certain things or having certain things. Or it can involve you being (or becoming) a certain sort of person. Or it can incorporate both. Second, there is the idea of a course of action for achieving this goal: the how-you-are-going-to-get-to-where-you-want-to-be aspect of the plan. To describe the plan as rational means that both elements can be rationally assessed. You can rationally assess your goal. Is being a professional footballer a realistic (i.e. broadly rational) goal around which to organize your life? This rational assessment can change over time. Is being a professional footballer a rational goal to pursue given that you are an overweight thirty-five-year-old man who hasn't played seriously since his teens? You can also assess the means for achieving the goal. Is yet another night at the pub the best way of pursuing your goal of becoming a professional footballer?

The idea of a rational plan for life is a version of the

A Design for Life

Socratic idea of an examined life. The idea of a rational life plan involves engaging in the critical scrutiny of both your goals and the means you choose to achieve these goals. In doing so, you pay careful attention to the facts on the ground and the likely consequences of your actions. Any realistic plan will be revisable in the light of emerging considerations of this sort: the facts are not what you thought they were, or you have changed your assessment of the likely consequences of your actions. In other words, having a rational life plan is not like supporting a football team, which may be highly irrational. Think of that time your dad takes you to watch Newport County when you are an unsuspecting four-year-old and, after the game, tells you:

'That's it. You support them now.'

'What, like forever, Dad?'

'I'm afraid so, my son. You're Port forever now.'

You may be condemned to a lifetime of frustration and misery by your father. But you don't have to condemn yourself to such a life through rigid adherence to a plan of your own that has proven unworkable.

Nevertheless, there are limits to how much you can revise your life's plan. Revise it too comprehensively, and you are now dealing with a new plan rather than with an amended version of the original one. Do it too often, and you are dealing with a succession of different plans, and the idea of a rational plan for life has evaporated. What this means for practical purposes is that, in general but with some exceptions, revisions to the plan must be forced rather than chosen. In general, that is to say, the plan is revised or abandoned only when this is forced upon the planner. You wake up on the morning of your fortieth birthday nursing yet another hangover, and realize your plan of becoming a professional footballer probably needs reassessment. Finding a suitable middle ground is the hard part. If revisions are too easy, then one plan quickly becomes another, which just as quickly transforms into another, and the whole idea of a rational life plan has gone out of the window. But if revisions are too difficult, then the plan will be cumbersome, non-adaptive, and not fit for purpose.

The idea that revisions must be severely constrained – generally forced rather than chosen, or (which may or may not be equivalent) chosen only after being forced – lies at the heart of what I think is the most serious problem with the idea of a rational plan for life. A rational plan for life tends to close you off to the myriad possibilities life has to offer. Many of the best and most important things that have happened in my life – and I'm talking of pretty much all of life's major landmarks – were accidents, either completely or in large part. Life can throw many things at you, and some of those things are opportunities. An undue focus on 'the plan' can make you insufficiently cognizant of all the other, unplanned, opportunities life contains.

Perhaps, then, the plan model needs revising. Instead of thinking in terms of life as a plan, we might be better advised to think of it as more akin to a *voyage*. In most voyages there is, of course, a destination, as well as

A Design for Life

some means of getting there. In this, a voyage resembles a plan. However, while the destination, or goal, of a plan is laid out in the plan itself – it's part of the plan – the destination of a voyage may be far less clear. You know it's going to end somewhere, but precisely where and when may not be specified in the voyage. And, anyway, there is far more to a voyage than the eventual destination, wherever that may be. The best part of a voyage – and, indeed, its point – can often be the travelling itself. Encountering people, events and things you didn't expect to encounter. Being surprised; being amazed; the delightful contingencies and the unexpected opportunities – the things you never planned for: these may be the best parts of the voyage.

The life of a dog is much more like a voyage than a plan. Of course, the dog's understanding of the voyage's destination may be hazy at best. But the same is true, to a greater or lesser extent, of us too. Having ceded most of his cognitive responsibilities to us, a dog does not plan. Not much, anyway. Any plans pertaining to his life will be drawn up by us. There are obvious drawbacks with this arrangement, but I think those are balanced by something else. What the dog has, and what those who are addicted to planning have lost, is a certain kind of spontaneity, together with the joy that accompanies it, that can only be found when there is no plan. In a few moments, when I complete this chapter and walk away from this laptop, I will see this spontaneity in Shadow, as I see it every day. 'What! Are you walking over to my leash? You're picking it up! We are going for a walk! F-ing A! Super happy! Super, super happy! Give me that leash! Let me take it over to the door for you!' This is a rough translation, of course, but his sentiments are clear. Not only clear, but repeated every day, every walk, as if it were the first walk, a walk in Eden. Contrast this with me, laden and leaden with plans. I have to pencil these walks into my schedule. I know exactly when and where they must occur. No surprises for me today. Unless we meet a moccasin on the canal bank. It is snake season, after all. Shadow's kind of spontaneity is lost to me. Not because I am old, and not because I am tired (although I am both of those things). Generally, but fundamentally, this kind of spontaneity is lost because I am a planner. Plans suck the life out of, well, life. They make of life a desiccated vessel.

I am all too human. Far too human to even consider turning all my planning over to someone else. But even I, the inveterate life planner, the cunning ape, can see that we have lost something in our meticulously planned out lives. A little less planning and a little more voyaging would probably do us all the good in the world. In our plans, we legislate for our future, our future selves and even our future desires. But in doing so, we risk legislating against all the surprises we would have had if we had walked towards that future more spontaneously. Time for a walk. Shadow, go and put on your leash, mate!

7

Just Dogs with the Yips

> If we take eternity to mean not infinite temporal duration but timelessness, then eternal life belongs to those who live in the present. Our life has no end in just the way in which our visual field has no limits.
>
> —Ludwig Wittgenstein, *Tractatus Logico-Philosophicus*

Hugo was a German shepherd too, and large like Shadow, but there the resemblance ended. When I remember Hugo now, the overriding theme of my memories is one of calm obligation. Hugo was an inordinately calm dog, even tempered, even keeled. His life was shaped not by aggression but by obligation, and also by love. He came into our lives when our oldest son was one year old, a year before the birth of our second. He formed a close bond with both of the boys. As a shepherd, he liked his flock to be together in one place, and if they diverged he would do his best to herd them back together – fun for them and utterly exhausting for him, of course, especially if they were running around in a field or on a beach. He was keenly attuned to the possibility of danger. Once when my wife and sons were walking along a street in the Croix-Rousse area of Lyon, he herded them away from the entrance to a restaurant. Seconds later a drunk man staggered out into what would have been their path. He was very good at that sort of thing. He was a dog with a keen eye and a strong sense of duty, which he discharged in an efficient, understated way.

There is an episode that I think nicely captures the essence of Hugo, of what he was all about. One summer, I had lined up a long list of talks I was going to give in various countries of Europe. We had flown over from the States for the summer, bringing Hugo with us. There was a reasonable amount of downtime between talks, and so one week saw us staying in a campsite just outside Rome. It was a good campsite, but in a somewhat dodgy area, although we didn't know that at the time. I had taken the boys to the water slides, and my wife and Hugo had stayed by the tent. My wife was sitting outside the tent, in a largely deserted site, numerous Apple devices strewn on the table in front of her, when three men appeared – we were later told by the camp staff that they were well-known local criminals. Who knows what would have happened next if Hugo hadn't come and sat next to my wife? Certainly robbery, and perhaps a lot worse. With a frosty stare at the men and a low growl issuing from his throat, which gradually increased in volume as the miscreants grew nearer, Hugo made the men stop and think about what

Just Dogs with the Yips

they were planning to do. My wife could see them discussing what to do – and they eventually thought better of it and went away. I know Hugo well enough to know that he would not have enjoyed that situation at all. Shadow would have thoroughly relished it I'm sure, but potentially violent confrontations were not Hugo's thing. He did his duty, however, his actions guided by an acute sense of obligation.

Hugo was from a West German line, as opposed to Shadow's East German working line. Neither actively nor reactively aggressive, Hugo harboured no overtly murderous impulses towards other dogs, ducks, humans or even iguanas. He did enjoy chasing squirrels, but I'm not sure he ever really understood why. He once trapped a young squirrel, cornered it in the pool fence, and then just stood there looking puzzled. 'Evidently, I haven't thought this through. What do I do now?' He wasn't too keen on running. In the winter months, he wasn't averse, but whenever he decided that it was too hot – which it frequently was most of the year in Miami – he would stand at the door and refuse to budge. 'No, you go on, mate. I'm going to stay in today.' Hugo had little interest in the canal and its residents, much preferring to hang out at home with my sons. The canal's iguanas that would one day play such an important role in Shadow's life left Hugo utterly unimpressed. But one thing that he did love was his bite sleeve. Or rather, sleeves: he worked his way through them with astonishing alacrity.

I remember his first sleeve, a 'Christmas present' for

him. As much for me as for him, I admit, and Santa may have delivered it slightly early (late summer, I seem to remember). He was around six months old at the time and had never seen a sleeve before, but somehow knew exactly what he was supposed to do with it. He had clamped his jaws around it before I had even finished removing it from the box. It was the beginning of a life-long obsession, and I mean that quite literally. In his early years, he would charge at me, the sleeve-bearer, with an intensity quite at odds with the dog who had spared the life of a young squirrel, and who refused to leave the comfort of his house because it was, all things considered, a little too warm outside. In those early years, in any given session, I would be knocked over on several occasions. Sometimes, when the sleeve was a little worn and needed upgrading, I could feel my bones crunching beneath his bite. He had a very strong bite. And my shoulder has never quite recovered from the beating it took. But as the years rolled on, this sort of rough and tumble slowly became too much for him (not to mention me). And in his final years, I would simply throw the sleeve for him to chase and retrieve. Pedestrian compared with his earlier efforts, certainly, but he still loved this with a passion. Even in those later years, there was nothing in the world he would rather do than chase his bite sleeve.

Hugo's end came on a dismal morning of the brightest sunshine, only a day after his tenth Christmas – a day that will forever ruin the festive period for my children. Christmas day had started cheerfully for all of us, but it took a notable turn for the worse that evening. Hugo could no longer bear the pain of his arthritic hips. The vet had warned me for some time that this day was coming, but the speed at which it finally unfolded was shocking. Christmas morning, he was fine, bouncing around the garden after his new sleeve – in the event, his last Christmas present. I suspected something was up when he went into the pool on his own that afternoon – something he had never done before. He sat there, almost submerged. I had made sure we had a large stockpile of painkillers for him in the house in case something like this happened over the holiday. By Boxing Day, even the copious amounts of painkillers and anti-inflammatories we had been giving him had seemed to have stopped working. All the veterinarian offices were closed for the holiday, but I managed to arrange for a mobile veterinarian to visit. The scene was set for Hugo's last act.

When I say Hugo could no longer bear the pain in his arthritic hips, I mean that even sitting or lying down was now too painful for him. Mercifully, this final stage of pain did not occur until the vet was practically on her way to the house. During those final hours, all he could do was stand, practically asleep on his feet with exhaustion. There may have been other factors or pathologies involved besides the arthritis: he was an old dog. But I'll never know. I do know, and will probably always remember, how his final hour unfolded.

The vet would soon arrive to put Hugo to sleep. My eyes brimming with tears, I decided to take Hugo out to the garden for him to say goodbye. He walked over to his sleeve, picked it up and brought it to me. Incredulous, I accepted it from him and gently tossed it a few paces. He jogged over, picked it up and brought it back to me again. The next time I threw it further. Hugo ran, faster this time, and again brought the sleeve back to me, his excitement discernibly growing. Soon he was sprinting, like the Hugo of old, the Hugo who was not doomed to die this day, within the hour.

Even now when I look back, I think, 'How could I do it?' How could I end the life of a dog who had been chasing around the garden a few short moments ago? Surely I must have been mistaken about his condition? I almost called the veterinarian. I almost told her not to come; that everything was all right, that Hugo had, somehow, miraculously recovered. But as soon as we returned to the house, after ten minutes of throwing and chasing, the mirage dissolved before my eyes. Hugo returned to the dying dog that he had been a short time before. The pain returned, too much pain to bear. Too much pain to lie down; too much pain to even sit down. He stood there, head hanging nearly to the ground, asleep on his feet. I hugged him, holding him up as best I could until the vet arrived. These moments haunt me. It is always difficult when you are called upon to end the life of a dog you love. He cannot tell you how bad things are, and often you will never really know if you got the timing right. Was it a day too early? A day too late? I know I was a day too late for Hugo. I let him down at the end. But those moments with the sleeve almost redeemed me. Fierce and free, in the grip of what he loved doing most in the world, he managed to hold death at bay, just for a while. Minutes from death, he had never looked more magnificent.

Professional philosophers, creatures who like to drain the magic out of life's most vibrant phenomena, have an expression they would apply to Hugo's behaviour: *subjective engagement*. This is a suitably bloodless term to capture myriad such wonders. It means that you like doing something. You find it enjoyable. Hugo, near death, bite sleeve clamped in his jaws, showed subjective engagement of a sort that I doubt any human could replicate. Hugo, the evidence seems clear, was in pain somewhere in the region between intense and indescribable. And yet – somehow – he managed to relegate this pain to the background of the irrelevant when an opportunity came along to do what he loved most in the world. That's the difference between Hugo and me. Here, people might talk of commitment – of how committed Hugo was to his avocation. Commitment is another suitably pallid term for what we are talking about. What we are talking about, of course, is love. The love of what you do.

I can't imagine ever loving an activity that much. There are certain things I like doing. I'm quite fond of running. Writing has always got the pulse racing too. Over the years, I have quite enjoyed watching Manchester United. Sex, yes, of course. But let's face it, none of these things that I enjoy are going to take away, even temporarily, the kind of pain we are talking about here. I can't think of anything that would. The lesson seems clear. I don't love things enough. Not as much as Hugo. Not my activities. Hugo loved what he did so much it could overwhelm immense pain, and even hold death at bay, if only for a while. There is nothing I do, no activity that might engage me, that I love as much as Hugo loved biting his sleeve.

Life, in the final analysis, is a sequence of activities – a linear series of things that we do and of things that happen to us. And so I am led to a seemingly inescapable conclusion. Hugo loved life more than I do. Hugo's love of life could neuter the kind of pain that most of us would say makes life not worth living. Hugo's love of life could even give death pause. I do not, and I suspect I cannot, love life this much. Why is this? Why do dogs love life so much more than we do? The answer, I think, is that life is always more precious for a dog than for a human because we have two lives and dogs only have one.

It's not that I am finding religion in my declining years. Not yet, anyway – who knows, maybe I'll get around to that eventually? I am not talking of this life and a life to come, a second life lived in a perfected heavenly state. Rather, we humans live our two lives simultaneously. We live them now, on earth rather than in heaven. There is the life we live from the inside, and there is the life we live from the outside. But for a dog, life is something lived ineluctably from the inside alone. There is only an inside to the life of a dog, and it is a life that has no limits – in the way that a visual field has no limits.

It is not possible, as Wittgenstein pointed out, to see the limit of your visual field. The limit of a visual field is where the seeing stops and not seeing begins. Things must be this way. If the limit of a visual field were within the field, and so was visible to you, then it wouldn't be a limit of that field but something within it. And something within a visual field cannot be the limit of that field. Similarly, Wittgenstein claims, death is not an event in life. If it were, it wouldn't be death. Death is the limit of a life and so cannot be part of that life, in the same way that the limit of a visual field cannot be part of that field. Unfortunately, however, this is only true of a life seen from the inside – a life as it is lived. Since dogs live only this sort of life, their life has no limits in Wittgenstein's sense. But it is not true of human lives. We live our lives from the inside and from the outside, simultaneously. And when viewed from the outside, life has clearly identifiable limits. Death is an event in a life viewed from the outside.

Unlike dogs, we humans are not just livers of lives, we are also watchers of those same lives. In our lives, we are not only actors, we are also spectators. As actors, we are immersed in our lives. But as spectators, we stand apart from them, watching, appraising, evaluating. As a result, like a bigamist husband with families on different sides of the country, we can never fully love either one of our two lives.

To understand the idea of these two lives, we can build on a distinction implicit in the earlier discussion of mirror self-recognition. This is a distinction between what we can call the *body-as-object* and the *body-as-lived*. The body-as-object is the body that you see in the mirror. It is the body you think about, the body for which you harbour hopes, and regarding which you have fears. I look in the mirror. The body I see is the object of my vision. If I think about this body, it becomes the object of my thought. Seeing and thinking are acts of consciousness – mental acts – and the body-as-object always exists as an object of these sorts of acts. That is, it exists as something these acts are about. There are many different types of mental act, of course, not just seeing and thinking. There is hoping, fearing, anticipating, wishing, and many more besides. But the body-as-object exists where there is a mental act and the body is an object of this act – it is what the act is about. Such acts as this all belong under a single, broader category of mental act. A mental act turned back on its author, or in this case the author's body, is a case of reflection. Thus, the body-as-object always exists as the object of an act of reflection. In effect, it is the body understood from the outside.

Just Dogs with the Yips

This body-as-object is a physical thing, with reasonably determinate spatial boundaries, marked by the skin, and reasonably determinate temporal boundaries, marked by birth and death. It has a certain size and a certain mass, and it has these properties in the same way that any other physical objects might have them. It is subject to generally well-understood physical laws. If this body were to fall off a cliff, it would, in the absence of any counteracting influences, fall with an acceleration of 9.8 m/s^2 – just like any other physical object. The body-as-object is, in short, a physical thing that obeys known physical laws of the universe.

The body-as-object is not the only way for the body to be. The body can exist in a very different way, a body-as-lived rather than a body-as-object. Most of the time – unless you suffer from crippling self-consciousness – you are not aware of your body as an object. Rather, you live through your body. You are aware of it only pre-reflectively, through your awareness of other things. You see a chair as one upon which you can sit, and a book as one you can reach. But you could neither sit on the chair nor reach the book if you were twelve inches tall. Seeing the chair and the book in this way – as sittable-upon, as reachable – therefore involves an implicit awareness of your body and its various dimensions and features. You are aware of your body through your awareness of these other things, specifically through the ways in which you are aware of these other things. This is pre-reflection, and through it you are aware of the body-as-lived.

The body-as-lived is not so much an object as an activity or process – a process of disclosure or revelation broadly understood. The chair that I see is revealed as empty, and therefore as sittable-upon. The book I need that sits on the table is revealed to be out of reach, and I must move to bring it within reach. It need not be out of reach for someone else – someone sitting at the table, for example. But it is out of reach for me. Pre-reflection arises through mental activity that reveals things as being a certain way relative to me. Pre-reflection makes me aware of myself through this relativity-to-me. But this relativity-to-me arises through a certain type of experience: revelation, experience through which things in the world are revealed as being a certain way. The body-as-lived is, therefore, revealing activity: activity through which things in the world are revealed as being a certain way rather than other ways: as sittable-upon, as reachable, as eatable or poisonous, as harmless or deadly, as fearsome or friendly, etc. The body-as-lived, therefore, is not a thing, not an object, but a process of worldly revelation. This body-as-lived is, we might say, the body understood from the inside, the body as it is lived rather than as it is seen or thought about.

🐾

Building on this distinction between the body-as-object and the body-as-lived, we can distinguish two perspectives that we can adopt to think about our lives. In effect, this means we humans live two lives. I am not, to reiterate, talking of a heavenly life to come after this one. There is *life-as-object* and *life-as-lived*. My life-as-object is the life I think about, about which I have hopes and fears, satisfaction and regret. It is my life viewed from the outside. Its temporal boundaries begin more or less at birth and culminate with my death. Its spatial boundaries are perhaps somewhat less clear, but my life takes place in the general vicinity of my body, it exists more or less where my body is. At present, for example, it is taking place in the general vicinity of Miami rather than in Milan or Maui or Mogadishu. My life-as-object is a series of events that I orchestrate or that happen to me, a sequence of actions and consequences, of successes, failures and things that fall somewhere in between. To capture this life-as-object, all I need do is delineate these sequences. 'Well, first I was born. That went okay, I suppose. And then a woman grabbed me by my ankles, turned me upside down and slapped my bottom, without so much as a by your leave . . .', and so on and so forth, for a very long time.

When I look at my life from the outside, I am forced to confront some uncomfortable truths. Just as my body-as-object is an unremarkable one, differing only in minor details from the bodies of others, so too is my life-as-object. I was born at a certain place and time and will similarly die at a certain place and time. In between, some things happened, and hopefully will continue to happen for the foreseeable future. But the result of all this is a life that is merely a minor variation on the life of any other human being, certainly no more significant than the life of any other. Any of my modest accomplishments, such as they are, will soon be washed away by time's remorseless tide. Any trace that I was ever here will quickly disappear. I am, in short, a finite, unremarkable creature of a finite, unremarkable species that lives, for a short time, in a remote and unremarkable corner of the universe. The medieval philosophers labelled this view of life as *sub specie aeternitatis*, the perspective of eternity: I am an insignificant speck in the great scheme of things, finite and mundane. We all are. This is the view of life-as-object. It is life viewed from the outside.

There is, however, another perspective on life, from which life is not so much viewed as it is lived. This is the view of life from the inside – the experience of life-as-lived. From this perspective, things appear very different. My life-as-lived matters. The things that happen in my life-as-lived matter – at least to me. And even if I were to try, I cannot stop them mattering. In this life-as-lived, there are goals that I cherish, and in which I might have invested years or decades of planning and hard labour. In this life-as-lived, there are achievements of which I am proud and failures of which I am ashamed. I cannot bring myself to regard my goals and plans, successes and failures as merely minor notational variants on those of others. In this life also are people I love, and even if I were to try, I cannot stop loving them. I know other people have their loves too, but mine are especially important to me. My life-as-lived is a hub of meaning and purpose, with every bump in the road a potential source of heartache, and every triumph, no matter how minor and temporary, an occasion for satisfaction.

Any human, then, has two lives. There is life-as-object and life-as-lived. We live both lives, and therefore can be fully immersed in neither of them. We flit continually between these perspectives. Just as life-as-lived pulls us in, holds us tight in its embrace, we can be ripped out of it by the newly assertive perspective of life-as-object. But to be immersed in life, to give oneself over to it, is a necessary condition of loving it. Hugo was immersed in his bite sleeve and the things he did with it. That is what it means to say he loved it. I can never be similarly immersed. The nagging tug of the perspective of life-as-object sees to that. Hugo had only one life and I have two. That is why he loved his life more than I love mine.

🐾

It is not only the love of a life that is at stake – its coherence is in jeopardy too. The problem is not simply that we humans have two perspectives on life. Rather, it is that these perspectives are of doubtful compatibility. It is, of course, perfectly possible to adopt two perspectives on the same thing. I can look at the same mountain from both the north and the south. I might not even realize these are perspectives on the same mountain. Indeed, sometimes it may seem unlikely that different perspectives can be perspectives on the same thing – as with the well-known allegory of three blindfolded people each being allowed to touch a different part of an elephant – one the trunk, one the tail and the other the body – without realizing they are all being presented with different perspectives on the same thing. The case of the two perspectives we can adopt on life, however, is different. It may seem unlikely to the three blindfolded people that they each have a perspective on the same thing. This is because what is revealed from each perspective seems so different from the others. However, the incompatibility between the two perspectives on life is deeper than this. It is not that it is merely unlikely they are both true. It seems impossible for them to both be true.

Both perspectives on life can't be true because they are incompatible with each other. To believe both would be to believe a contradiction, or so it seems. My life can't be unimportant and important, significant and insignificant, meaningless and meaningful. Usually, when one recognizes that one holds incompatible beliefs, one tries to excise at least one of them. But that option doesn't seem to be available in this case. I cannot rid myself of the view from the outside, of my life-as-object, because, among other things, I am pretty sure it is true. I am indeed an unremarkable creature living an unremarkable life in an unremarkable way. Perhaps, then, I should try to dispense with the view of my life-as-lived. However, that, for me at least, and I suspect for most others, is psychologically impossible, requiring a depth of nihilism that is beyond my capacity, and beyond the capacity of most of us. I can't stop things mattering to me, I can't stop caring about the things that happen in my life, and I suspect most other people will find themselves in the same boat. This is the problem, then. The two perspectives on life are mutually incompatible. They can't both be true. We know this. But we can't bring ourselves to abandon either one of them. Any creature that adopts these two perspectives on its own life must, it seems, be existentially confused — confused about the nature of its existence. We are such creatures. This is what some — influenced by the important work of the philosopher Thomas Nagel — have come to understand as the *absurdity* of the human condition.

In this understanding of absurdity, for one's life to be absurd, one needs to be able to adopt both perspectives on life — the perspective of life-as-lived and that of life-as-object. But the latter perspective is available only to creatures capable of reflection. It is likely, therefore, that this problem of absurdity afflicts only humans. If it arises in other creatures at all, it will only do so in a significantly attenuated — essentially negligible — form. While some other species have some capacity for reflection, only humans have raised this kind of awareness into a species-defining obsession. A dog does not suffer from this affliction. A dog cannot adopt the view from the outside on its life. A dog cannot make its life into an object, and therefore cannot see its life as just one life among many others, no more remarkable than that of any other dog. The only view a dog has of its own life is the view from the inside. It understands only life-as-lived. In a dog's life, there is no absurdity. The lives of dogs make sense. Ours, not so much.

Much human philosophy, since its inception, has been an attempt to integrate these perspectives: to merge the view of us from the inside with the view of us from the outside. What am I? What is the relation between my mind and my body? Do I have free will? How much can I know? Indeed, can I know anything at all? What is morally good and what is bad? These questions, and many more variations on these general themes, can all, in one way or another, be traced back, by routes straight or circuitous, to this division between the view from the inside and the view from the outside, between life-as-lived and life-as-object. The results of more than two thousand years of earnest endeavour in addressing these problems have been disappointing. There is no universally accepted resolution – and typically not even a widely accepted one – of any of these problems arising from this clash of perspectives. Our lives still don't make sense. There is nothing much about us that does.

It is time to recognize that these problems are neither universal nor inevitable. They are not questions woven into the objective fabric of the universe, arising equally for all creatures in all places and times. They arise only for a particular, and rather peculiar, creature. They are best viewed as an affliction of this creature only. These problems are, in other words, a bit like measles. Measles erupted in the human population in the thirteenth century, a mutant form of the rinderpest virus that was endemic in sheep and goats. In its nascent form, it was a particularly nasty virus, the cause of tens of millions of deaths. But then it settled down in its host, mutating to become an exclusively human virus, and becoming a lot less lethal in the process. It still kills tens of thousands annually, with sub-Saharan Africa taking the brunt of these deaths, but it is nothing like the threat it used to be in years gone by.

No matter how lethal it is in humans, it would be quixotic to introduce an initiative aimed at curing measles in other animals, for no other animals can get it. The virus has evolved into an exclusively human pathogen. Philosophy is a little like measles. No other animals can catch it, for no other animal can be absurd in the way humans can. In the days of its youthful virulence it killed Socrates, but that was over two thousand years ago. The philosophy with which I am acquainted, the philosophy taught in schools and colleges and published in journals and books, the philosophy that gets you tenure at universities, probably isn't going to kill anyone any more. Benign neglect seems to be the appropriate way of treating it. Dogs get parvo, we get philosophy. But whereas parvo is serious, and widespread vaccination essential, philosophy is really not that dangerous. Don't take it too seriously. Don't worry about it. Let it run its course. It will all work out in the end.

Do you see what I just did? I took the view from the outside on philosophy – the view of philosophy-as-object rather than philosophy-as-lived. In the end, it won't work. Philosophy is a little like a rash. Certainly, you can look at it from the outside. It is a minor, utterly unremarkable rash. Just ignore it and it will go away. The problem is that you can't ignore it. You can't ignore it because it itches. Philosophy is like a persistent and irritating rash. From the outside, innocuous, but from the inside, maddening. In this, philosophy is a not entirely inappropriate allegory for human life.

🐾

What philosophy is not, however, is a good allegory for the life of a dog. When we humans try to capture the kind of unadulterated commitment to an activity, of the sort exhibited by Hugo, instead of philosophy, our appeal is often to sports, or to play more generally. At their best, sports are a place where we can love life. In taking part in sports, adults can sometimes approximate – never emulate, I suspect, only approximate – the commitment of dogs. Children are better at it than we are. When the philosopher Moritz Schlick – surprisingly, for those familiar with the general tenor of his work – wrote, 'The meaning of life is play,' what he had in mind by 'play' was absorption in an activity that seeks no external reward or validation, an activity that is done for its own sake rather than for any other benefits it might bestow on the player. Like chasing and retrieving a bite sleeve, for example. But if play is the meaning of life, we humans suffer from an illness to which dogs and, for the most part, children seem to be immune. This illness goes by several names. *Choking* and *the yips* might be the most common. Whatever we call it, this is a disease born of reflection.

Choking and the yips are often run together, but for my purposes it is useful to distinguish between them. Choking, as I understand it, is a more general phenomenon than the yips. Choking denotes a general collapse in the face of pressure exerted on you by an opposition player or team. Often, this happens when the stakes are high. Think of Jana Novotná against Steffi Graf in Wimbledon 1993, two games away from victory, only for her game to crumble. Or Chelsea's John Terry in the 2008 Champions League penalty shootout with Manchester United. (Okay, I know, the grass was slippery.)

The yips, as I shall use this expression, is a specific form that choking may take, and centrally involves reflection. The term 'the yips' was first introduced by champion golfer Tommy Armour to describe certain difficulties he experienced, including uncontrollable wrist spasms that occurred when he was preparing to make a putt. Since then, its use has broadened considerably to encompass any loss of ability to execute the core motor skills of a sport. It may be that the use of the expression has become so broad that it no longer picks out a single phenomenon but, rather, refers to several different ones. I am going to focus on one of these phenomena. As I shall use the expression, 'the yips' denotes a decline in performance that stems from an undue focus on what one is doing. If one focuses too much on the details of technique and execution, rather than simply getting on with the business of playing, then one is suffering from the yips in the sense employed here. The result of the yips is a kind of paralysis through analysis, and one's performance levels drop significantly. Golfers seem particularly susceptible to this, but the phenomenon is also prevalent in other highly technical sports, such as cricket, baseball and darts. However, perhaps the most important thing to understand about the yips is that it is not essentially a sporting phenomenon. That is, its sporting incarnation is just one instance of a much wider phenomenon. Far from being restricted to athletic endeavours, the yips, in the above sense, are an *existential* characteristic of human beings, a feature of human existence more generally. The yips are an affliction caused by reflection. When this affliction occurs outside of sporting contexts, it often goes by another name: shame.

When Adam and Eve ate the apple of the tree of knowledge of good and evil, they experienced shame for the first time – becoming aware of their nakedness, among other things, and doing their best to cover it up. The essence of shame lies in the experience of oneself as an object for another. Sartre provides a nice illustration: 'Let us imagine that moved by jealousy, curiosity, or vice I have just glued my ear to the door and looked through a keyhole. I am alone and on the level of a non-thetic self-consciousness ... there is no self to inhabit my consciousness ... [my acts] are in no way known; I *am my acts* [emphasis in original].' We can perhaps overlook the difficult logistics involved in simultaneously peeking through a keyhole while gluing your ear to the door. This descriptive infelicity aside, we all understand the situation Sartre is describing. I am looking through a keyhole at a scene I really should not be looking at. I am absorbed in the scene – that's where all my attention is focused – and so I am not thinking about what I am doing. This is what he means by 'there is no self to inhabit my consciousness ... I am my acts'. I am pre-reflectively aware of myself – because pre-reflection comes with any conscious experience – but not reflectively self-aware.

This voyeuristic situation, however, rapidly changes: 'But all of a sudden I hear footsteps in the hall. Someone is looking at me. ... I am suddenly affected in my being and ... essential modifications appear in my structure ... I am for myself only as I am a pure reference to the Other.' Before I hear the footsteps, I am the subject of my experience. The scene behind the door unfolds before my eyes and takes place in an egocentric space that is ultimately arranged around me. The scene is unfolding in front of me. One element of the scene is slightly to my left, while another is slightly to my right. With the arrival of the other person, this all changes. Now, I experience myself as an object for the other. Before the appearance of the other person, I am utterly absorbed in the scene unfolding behind the door. But when I hear footsteps, I now experience myself as I think I must appear to the other person – as a voyeur, hunched over a keyhole. I experience myself as an object in his visual field; he is now the centre of my experience, not me.

This experience of oneself as an object for the other, Sartre calls *shame*: 'the Other is the indispensable mediator between myself and me. I am ashamed of myself *as I appear* to the Other. By the mere appearance of the Other, I am put in the position of passing judgment on myself as on an object, for it is as an object that I appear to the Other ... Shame is by nature *recognition*. I recognize that I am as the Other sees me ... [S]hame is shame *of oneself before the Other.*'

Most of the time, mercifully, we don't experience ourselves in this way. To do so would be a symptom of pathology – perpetually in the position of the hapless overly self-conscious public speaker on a stage giving a speech, crippled by thoughts of how he must appear to the audience. In these circumstances, the unfortunate speaker relates to his body as an object – he sees himself as he thinks the other sees him. The standard advice – imagine the audience in their underwear – is an attempt to change the focus of your experience – to force the object of your awareness to swivel from you to them, with you consequently being reasserted as the subject of experience. Most of the time, happily, one does not experience one's body as an object of awareness. Rather, as we have seen, one lives *through* one's body. Or better: *you live your body.*

Nevertheless, experiencing yourself as an object for the other is something that is available to us humans because of our capacity for reflection. To regularly experience yourself in this way would be a sign that something has gone very wrong in your life. If you spend a significant portion of your life imagining how others must see you or think of you then you have problems. If you spend significant portions of the day looking in the mirror, you also have problems. If you spend much of your time agonizing about your life and where it is heading, your problems might be less obvious, but they may be no less real. Undue focus on yourself is a sign that somewhere along the line things have gone wrong. You would be suffering from the generalized, existential form of the yips. An undue focus on your life will stymie that life, prevent it going where you would like it to go. It is about as good for your life as the yips are for a golfer about to take the decisive putt on the last hole of the Masters.

I don't want to claim that all other animals are simply incapable of reflection. Some may be capable of this to some extent. However, if they have it at all, their capacity for reflection is Lilliputian in comparison with ours. We humans are the undisputed world heavyweight champions of reflection, and its exercise appears in our life with a regularity that can only be described as pathological. No other creature has availed itself of reflection in the way, and to the extent, that we have. That is why we are so miserable. That is why our lives are absurd. That is why our lives can appear, and perhaps actually be, bereft of meaning. Reflection is the death of commitment, and commitment is just another word for love. The pathological overuse of our ability for self-reflection, therefore, tears love out of our lives.

We can only dream of the love of Hugo. Old and dying, but still utterly in love with what he was doing. Compared with Hugo, we are like children with iPhones, continually flitting from one TikTok video to the next. Doubt is the child of reflection and dissatisfaction the child of doubt. We humans, as I have mentioned already, have long desired to adequately define ourselves, without notable success: we have called ourselves featherless bipeds, rational [*sic*] animals, *Homo ludens* even – as if other animals do not play. This desire for self-definition is probably just another sign of pathology. Nevertheless, sickly human animal that I am, I'm afraid I can't resist offering another one. Perhaps the safest general definition of humans is this: we are all just dogs suffering from the yips.

8

Sometimes Toward Eden

Sometimes toward Eden, which now in his view
Lay pleasant, his grieved look he fixes sad.

—John Milton, *Paradise Lost*

There will be storms later this afternoon, but for now, on this morning in early June, there is blue sky from the Atlantic to the Everglades. Shadow's decline is as clear as this sky. I walk with two Shadows every day. There is the Shadow who trots beside me, and there is the Shadow of my scattered notes and drafts from which this book has gradually emerged. The contrast is jarring. The Shadow that walks with me still scatters our iguanas to the winds, but when I slip the leash, I know he can no longer guarantee the quarter-mile explosion of yesteryear. One hundred yards, maybe two, and his mind turns to other things. He still swears profusely at the iguanas as he drives them into the water. At least I assume that is what all the growling is about – a stream of invective, liberally spiced with canine profanities. But he is fading. Perhaps our iguanas have come to recognize this.

The Happiness of Dogs

I know my own decline must mirror his, but there is no record of this in my notes. I live my decline rather than see it. It is the intensity that goes first. Being a writer is not so much about talent, although I always wished I had a bit more. It's not even about hard work understood in a scattergun, one-size-fits-all way. It is the intensity you bring that is crucial. I used to write in eight-hour stretches, just to set up the hours that would follow. Nothing much happens in the first eight hours. You can do some neat little technical work in those hours, some incremental improvements here and there. But it's when you are exhausted, when your thoughts are tired and no longer recognize their customary, agreed-upon rules and avenues, when they start stumbling down paths they never would have travelled down if your brain was working properly – that is when the interesting things happen. Writing, for me, always had a touch of the ultra about it. It was a life of marathons that you would run just to get to the miles that would come when the marathon was over. Muhammad Ali was once asked how many sit-ups he did. He replied, 'I don't know. I don't start counting until it starts hurting.' Writing only really begins when it starts to hurt.

How much hurt I have left in me, I don't know. You never know whether the intensity is still there until one day it's not. Can you keep going, with your heart hammering and your legs failing, beyond two hundred yards, force out three, grind out four? Can you keep going as you hear the panicked scurrying of reptiles and the gratifying splash as they hit the water? Brenin was the dog of my youth – an extended childhood that continued well into my mid-thirties. In most important respects, I grew up with Brenin. But Shadow is the dog with whom I grew old. He is my friend who kept me company as we began walking towards or along – the distinction has no real meaning – that avenue dark, nameless and without end. This is a debt I owe Shadow; one that I will never be able to repay.

Shadow's dominion may be slipping, but his life seems as meaningful as ever. (That's one of the good things about a meaningful life: it doesn't require you to be at your best.) I began writing this book about what I saw as Shadow's decisive response to the challenge of Sisyphus. Its decisiveness puzzled me – and most of what I have written has started out as a puzzle somewhere – as I don't think humans have ever been able to decisively answer the challenge of Sisyphus. How is it that a dog, who doesn't even know what the challenge is, can answer it, while a human can invest a lifetime of thought without dealing it a glancing blow? The answer is that dogs never fell. We humans left Eden long ago, but they never did.

As a result of our fall, we live two lives. In one we are actors, indeed, the principal protagonists, in stories that are unquestionably ours. But in the other, we are spectators; onlookers and judges of a life that differs from the lives of others only in minor details. Because we have two lives, we are never conclusively immersed in either. As a result, we can never love either of these lives completely. We are creatures of doubt rather than creatures of love. But Shadow, who has only one life, knows what it is to love it.

🐾

Many think that only human lives can be meaningful. Those who think this are invariably human. Sometimes this belief is the result of religious predilections. The Christian philosopher William Lane Craig claims, 'If there is no God, then our life is not qualitatively different from that of a dog.' I initially took this as a compliment, but then realized that Craig does not appear to be a huge fan of dogs and did not mean this comparison in a good way. By this claim, then, we should probably take him to mean that without God, and the purpose he gives us, our lives are utterly lacking in meaning or significance. But non-religious people often cleave to this kind of human exceptionalism too. Secular humanism, when you get down to the brass tacks, is all about how great – indeed, exceptional – humans are, and about just how much they don't need a God in order for them to be this way. While the lives of animals can be enjoyable or miserable, replete with pleasure or pain, only human lives, many people seem to think, can be meaningful. I am convinced the opposite is true. Meaning comes effortlessly to the lives of dogs. For us it is hard work, seldom achieved with any sort of resounding satisfaction. You wish, William Lane Craig, that your life could be as meaningful as a dog's.

Sometimes Toward Eden

Philosophers, creatures who take delight in distinctions that would merely annoy anyone else, distinguish the question of the meaning *of* life from that of meaning *in* life. The consensus is that there is no meaning of life, in the sense of some grand purpose that would give human life meaning. We weren't put here for a reason – to achieve some purpose – neither individually nor collectively. For a start, us being put here for a reason would seem to require a God, and many people, William Lane Craig notwithstanding, don't believe in that sort of thing any more. But even if God existed and went to the trouble of assigning us a purpose, this wouldn't, by itself, be enough to put meaning in our lives. It all depends on the purpose. Only certain purposes will do.

In *Doctor Faustus*, Christopher Marlowe imagines a scenario in which God creates humans for his entertainment and that of his angels. He makes a wager with the angels that he can create a species whose lot is unutterably miserable and yet who will still worship him. God and the angels watch the unfolding train wreck that is the existence of humanity. In the final scene, God causes a star to smash into Earth. He mutters, 'That was a good play. I must have it played again.' If you and I were created for the entertainment of celestial beings, that would be the meaning of our lives in the sense of its purpose. But this purpose would not supply meaning in our lives. On the contrary, if you discovered that this was your purpose, how would you feel? It turns out that you are, essentially, a character in a divine version of *The Truman Show*. The discovery would quite possibly reduce meaning in your life rather than enhance it. You realize that you are a sucker, and that your life was never your own. A purpose assigned to you by God will give your life meaning only if you endorse or embrace it. Then, however, it is not so much the purpose that is important but your embracing, or endorsement, of it.

It is unlikely that we are characters on a heavenly stage built for the entertainment of celestial beings. It is unlikely that our lives have any grand purpose, not a purpose that is imposed on us by an outside agency such as God. If this is so, there is no meaning of life. However, current philosophical orthodoxy has it that there can still be meaning in life. Meaning in life is meaning understood from the perspective of the person who lives it rather than as assessed by reference to some outside purpose or plan. What this meaning is, and how some lives come to have it while others do not, is, to say the least, not entirely clear.

Any account of meaning in life must, I think, still define itself in relation to Albert Camus's seminal discussion of the myth of Sisyphus. 'Killing yourself,' Camus claimed, 'amounts to confessing. It is confessing that life is too much for you or that you do not understand it. Let's not go too far in such analogies, however, but rather return to everyday words. It is merely confessing that that "is not worth the trouble."' This suggests a simple formulation of the question of life's meaning: what makes life worth the trouble? However, the apparent simplicity of this formulation masks an ambiguity. The question could be understood descriptively or it could be understood prescriptively: as a description of how things are or as a prescription for how things should be. Understood descriptively, the question is this: what in fact makes life worth the trouble? Understood prescriptively, on the other hand, the question is subtly different: what should make life worth the trouble? Today, the two main competing accounts of meaning in life reflect this ambiguity in Camus's fundamental question.

One of these accounts is a subjectivist one. The things that make life worth living – and so provide meaning in that life – are activities that engage you, ones that you find attractive, activities that grip you. The word 'enjoyment' is often used to describe such activities, although this would have to be understood broadly, to cover a variety of experiential states. There is the enjoyment of sex, and the enjoyment of grimly grinding out the middle miles of a marathon. The notion of attraction, grip or engagement is intended to be broad enough to cover all these cases. According to subjective accounts, having meaning in life is a matter of being subjectively engaged in – attracted to, gripped by – what you do. That's all there is to it. If you want to know what makes life worth the trouble, all you need do is list activities of this sort.

The other main account is known as a *hybrid theory*. According to hybrid theories, subjective engagement, on its own, is not enough for meaning in life. In addition to merely being engaged in what you do, the things that engage you must be worthy of your engagement – not just in your opinion, but objectively so. As far as life's meaning is concerned, it is important to be engaged only by things that should engage you. As the philosopher Susan Wolf, a prominent advocate of this account, puts it, meaning in life arises when subjective attraction meets objective attractiveness. Meaning in life exists where your subjective engagement in what you do and the objective worth of what you do coalesce.

Logically, there is room for another account – a purely objectivist account, according to which meaning in life only requires that you perform activities that are objectively worthy. Such a view has few adherents, and it is not difficult to understand why. Suppose you spend your entire life trying to do something that everyone will likely accept is objectively valuable, like trying to find a cure for cancer or trying to end world hunger. However, you hate every single minute of this. Every morning when you wake, you are filled with dread and a visceral loathing of the day to come, and this only subsides when sleep mercifully claims you at the end of the day. Then, however, come the dreams. In every minute of your life, waking or sleeping, you long for death. Every breath you take you hope will be your last. Your life might be a good one in one sense. It is a noble one, defined by self-sacrifice of an especially dramatic sort. But it is not, conventional philosophical wisdom tells us, a meaningful one. There is goodness in it – indeed, goodness of an especially dramatic sort – but not meaning.

The debate among philosophers, therefore, has largely been over which one of two main competing theories is preferable: the purely subjectivist account, or the alternative hybrid theory. The problem is that both accounts face devastating objections.

The standard objection to subjectivist accounts is that one might in principle be subjectively engaged by any number of things, many of which might be completely banal, pointless or trivial – not the sort of activities, in other words, that could make one's life meaningful. We might call this the *Anorak Objection*. For non-British readers, an anorak, in the relevant sense, is not a type of coat but a person who is obsessively interested in a thing or topic that doesn't seem to anyone else to warrant such attention. Consider the case of Derek Anorak, a man obsessively interested in trainspotting. Derek spends a substantial portion of his life sitting beside isolated railway lines. His goal is to record various features of the trains that pass him, such as their make, model and engine number. This obsession, let us suppose, has taken over much of his life to an extent that he has abandoned friends, family and career. Derek is subjectively gripped by his avocation; indeed, there is little else in life that grips him. Nevertheless, many would argue, it is far from clear that his life is a meaningful one. If this intuition is correct, we cannot understand meaning in life simply in terms of subjective engagement. We need more than this; we need to be engaged in tasks that are objectively valuable. That is, we need a hybrid explanation of meaning in life.

I think there is something to this objection, but not exactly what those who wield it imagine. As stated, I think the objection exudes the distinctive bouquet of snobbery, intellectual or otherwise. Moreover, philosophically, the argument employs one of the oldest tricks in the book: introducing irrelevant considerations just to lead your interlocutor to the conclusion you want them to reach. Driving the intuitions that this argument tries to elicit is not Derek's trainspotting as such, but all the things he has neglected in the pursuit of this hobby. You could run the same argument for practically any activity. There goes Rowlands again. Writing another book. Neglecting his wife, neglecting his kids, lost his job because he failed to show up to teach. And even if the book is any good, everyone will have forgotten about it in no time at all. What a waste of a life. I admit, in the circumstances described, this might well be a questionable way to spend a life. However, apart from the 'writing a book' and possibly the 'everyone will have forgotten about it in no time at all' bits, this is all, mercifully, counterfactual. But even if my life was as described here, one cannot legitimately conclude that writing a book has no value. A more reasonable conclusion would be that writing a book is only one thing that has value, and its value can be outweighed by the loss of value of other things in life that one neglects while writing.

We might therefore make Derek a little more of a balanced individual. Trainspotters, we might point out, are not typically isolated individuals. Instead, they form clubs, and in these friendships naturally develop. Suppose also that Derek doesn't eschew family. On the contrary, he has a happy family that he helps support by means of his job, one that he doesn't particularly like, but that he does anyway to ensure a roof over his family's head and food on their table. In short, Derek has friends whose company he likes and a family he loves and helps support via his career. But he also has this thing he likes doing: spotting trains. He's not sure why he likes it so much, but he does. Now, ask yourself, is Derek's trainspotting worthless? On what grounds could we say that it is, other than because we don't like it, or think it is stupid? And why should Derek care what we think?

I think academics would be well advised to avoid hobby shaming wherever possible. Nevertheless, the Anorak Objection is, I think, not entirely without merit. Happily, I think I can identify its merits without insulting people's avocations. The core insight underlying the objection is this: we wouldn't want to make meaning in life too easy to achieve. Suppose that, as long as you liked doing it, anything you did, no matter what, was enough to give your life meaning. If this was so, then there would be no real content to the idea of meaning in life. Meaning in life would be ubiquitous, easily found wherever someone was doing something they enjoyed. It would be a trivial feature of almost all human lives, as easy to attain as breathing. Closely related to this worry is another one. When we talk about meaning in life, there must be at least the possibility of error. That is, it must be possible for any given person to be mistaken about whether their life is meaningful. It must at least be possible to think that your life is meaningful when it is not, or to think that it is not meaningful when it is. We can't, in other words, be infallible judges of whether our lives have meaning. If there is no possibility of error, the idea of meaning in life does not really mean very much at all. Both worries – ubiquity and infallibility – point in the same direction. We need some restrictions on which activities can make a life meaningful. This is precisely where the hybrid theorist will step in.

One advantage of the hybrid theory's appeal to objective value is that it can accommodate these two requirements of a theory of meaning in life. Meaning, according to this theory, requires engagement in activities that are objectively valuable. You can be mistaken about whether your life has meaning to the extent that you can be mistaken about whether your activities are objectively valuable. This avoids the infallibility problem. Moreover, so this theory goes, meaning is not found through joyous engagement in just any old activity but only in the ones that are objectively valuable. This avoids the ubiquity problem. Avoiding these problems is a distinct advantage of the hybrid theory. However, this is more than outweighed by its drawbacks. The primary problem with the hybrid theory is straightforward: those who advocate this theory really have no idea what they are talking about. This is because the core of the theory – the idea of objectively valuable activity – has no coherent meaning.

It is clear that we value things. It is clear that different people value different things. And it is clear that we value different things in different ways. These are all utterly mundane claims – but they are claims about valuing rather than about value. Valuing is an act. What is valued is the object of that act. When we value something we often say that it has value. This, however, raises a question almost as old as philosophy itself. Does something have value only because we value it? Or do we value it only because it has value?

If you think that something has value only because we value it, you are what is known as a constructivist about value. Constructivists think that value can be understood purely in terms of acts of valuing – that the notion of value is a 'construction' out of acts of valuing. Ultimately, there are simply acts of valuing, and everything we want to say about value can be said in terms of such acts. Constructivism is a version of subjectivism: valuing an activity is a way of being subjectively engaged with it. Conversely, the hybrid theory of life's meaning is committed to the idea that the value of something can be independent of (our acts of) valuing it. If something has value – of the sort that might lend meaning to a life – then it does so in itself, whether we value it or not. The hybrid theory, in other words, is committed to an objectivist view of value. According to this, the activities that give our lives meaning have value independently of their being valued by us. These activities are not made valuable by our valuing them. Rather, we value them precisely because they are valuable – objectively so, independently of whatever we happen to think about them.

The Achilles heel of objectivism has always been its attempt to make sense of the idea of objective value – value that exists independently of our acts of valuing. This is why constructivism has been by far the more popular view in recent times. This is not to say that it is correct. Fashions change. But it does mean that when a hybrid theorist throws in her lot with the objectivist camp, she is endorsing a controversial view, and is under a fairly pressing burden to explain what she means by objective value. This, however, is a difficult, perhaps impossible, undertaking.

To see the kinds of difficulties involved, consider an appeal to objective value in another domain. I have, let us suppose, written a book. Not this current one that I am now scribbling away at, but some other imaginary book. I believe this book to be a towering literary triumph – not just in my opinion, but objectively so. Who cares if everyone else thinks it banal, derivative and, generally, varying degrees of execrable? Some might think it likely that I am wrong and everyone else is right. But I am unperturbed by its reception because I believe in objective literary value and maintain that my book has this even if everyone else fails to recognize it. Even when I die – a bitter, unfulfilled death, no doubt – and there is no one left in the world who thinks the book is any good, it will still be. Objective literary worth, you see.

This scenario, at my expense, is intended to make clear just how mysterious the appeal to objective literary value is. What is objective literary value? In virtue of precisely what do some things have it while other things do not? Why does my book have it? If I am unable to answer these questions – and answer them in a way that shows I am not just reciting my subjective prejudices – then I really have no idea what objective literary value is. The appeal to such value is therefore without merit. It is an appeal to something I do not understand.

For the hybrid theorist, matters are, if anything, even worse. In the above example, at least I knew the genre of value to which I was appealing – literary value – even if I couldn't explain what this value was or why certain works had it. But when the meaning of life is at issue, it is not even clear what genre of value is being invoked. Other familiar genres of value do not seem to fit the case of life's meaning. Some might think we could use the concept of moral value. Of course, there are serious difficulties involved in understanding this in objectivist terms. But even if we could get around these problems – which, for the record, we probably can't – the appeal to moral value would lead to an implausible moralization of the idea of meaning in life. The problem is that meaning and morality don't seem to cohere particularly closely. Intuitively, immoral lives – indeed, even thoroughly despicable lives – can be meaningful ones. When Attila the Hun built a vast empire from east of the Volga to deep into Western Europe – at its height as far as Gaul – he used methods that were, to say the least, morally questionable. But it would be implausible to deny that his life was meaningful. If Attila's life was not meaningful, then whose life is? The same can be said for all empire builders. Julius Caesar, in his role in the expansion of the Roman Empire, followed by his eventual return to Rome to assume the role of dictator, also arguably employed methods as morally dubious as Attila's. But, again, if we refuse to count his life as meaningful, whose life would qualify as such? I suspect it is comparatively rare for people to have statues erected to them unless they were in some way a bit morally questionable, and sometimes morally execrable. But it would be far-fetched to deny that the lives of such people were meaningful. Meaning in life is not essentially a moral phenomenon. You don't have to be good to lead a meaningful life. You don't have to be bad either, of course, But if you are bad, this in no way disqualifies you from leading such a life.

Sometimes Toward Eden

The hybrid theorist's appeal to objective value as a way of explaining meaning in life is, therefore, an appeal shrouded in mystery. It is genuinely unclear what this appeal means and, indeed, whether it has any meaning at all. Susan Wolf, a prominent hybrid theorist, acknowledges the difficulties involved in explaining the idea of objective value, but doubles down on the idea, claiming that if we don't assume that at least some things have objective value, life can have no meaning. However, rather than explaining what objective value is, or would be, and why it attaches to some things and not others, Wolf employs a more indirect strategy. She points to a collection of activities, some of which (she thinks) are clearly meaningful, some of which (she thinks) are clearly meaningless, and some of which are indeterminate. The idea is that the distinction between meaningful and meaningless activities reliably tracks, or corresponds to, the distinction between objectively valuable and objectively worthless activities. That is, the activities we will judge to be meaningful are ones with objectively valuable goals, and the ones we judge to be worthless are ones with objectively worthless goals. If we can reliably distinguish meaningful from meaningless activities, she argues, we must have at least some understanding of the difference between objectively worthy and objectively worthless activities.

In Wolf's eyes, meaningless activities include collecting rubber bands, memorizing the dictionary, making handwritten copies of great novels, riding

The Happiness of Dogs

roller coasters, meeting movie stars, watching sitcoms, playing computer games, solving crossword puzzles, recycling, and writing cheques to Oxfam and the ACLU (it is not the giving she regards as meaningless but the mechanical process of filling in and signing the cheques). Meaningful activities, on the other hand, include moral or intellectual accomplishments, personal relationships, religious practices, mountain climbing, training for a marathon, and helping a friend. She also lists cases somewhere in between – those which are, in her view, neither obviously meaningful nor obviously meaningless. These include a life obsessed with corporate law, being devoted to a religious cult, and being a pig farmer who buys more land to grow more corn to feed more pigs to make more money to buy more land, and so on (the last one is, essentially, a version of Sisyphus, where he becomes a pig farmer instead of a rock roller).

Far from clarifying the issue, I think these lists only cloud it further and show how difficult it is to make sense of the idea of objective value. Training for a marathon is meaningful but playing computer games is not. Why? What if I am training for a *Beat Saber* marathon? Religious practices are meaningful, but if those practices veer in the direction of the cult-like, they become candidates for meaningless activities. To those who suspect there is a little of the cult in all religious practices, this may be surprising. Helping a friend is meaningful, but helping the planet by recycling is not? Mountain climbing is objectively valuable, but riding roller coasters is not – try telling that to my sons. More than anything, when I look at Wolf's lists, I can see only the prejudices of a successful middle-class, goal-driven professional academic.

The hybrid theorist's appeal to the objective value of some activities faces a further problem. Not only is it controversial, and not only is it inherently mysterious, but it is also arguably useless – at least when deployed in the context of questions about the meaning of life. When such questions are raised, the appeal to objective value is ineffective because anxieties that might lead a person to question whether his life is meaningful are often intimately entangled with anxieties about the objective worth of what he does. In this passage from his short book *A Confession*, Tolstoy provides a striking example of this entanglement:

> Amid the thoughts of estate management which greatly occupied me at that time, the question would suddenly occur: 'Well, you will have 6,000 *desyatínas* of land in Samára Government and 300 horses, and what then?' ... And I was quite disconcerted and did not know what to think. Or when considering plans for the education of my children, I would say to myself: 'What for?' Or when considering how the peasants might become prosperous, I would suddenly say to myself: 'But what does it matter to me?' Or when thinking of the fame my works would bring me, I would say to myself, 'Very well; you will be more famous than Gógol or

Púshkin or Shakespeare or Molière, or than all the writers in the world – and what of it?' And I could find no reply at all.

In this passage, Tolstoy is not merely questioning whether his activities and achievements have objective value; more fundamentally, he is questioning the idea of objective value itself: whether anything has it and, indeed, whether there even is such a thing. Tolstoy's anxieties about whether his life has meaning are inseparable from his worries about the objective worth of his – or anyone's – achievements. Therefore, I doubt Tolstoy would be very satisfied with Wolf's claim that we must assume there is such a thing as objective value, and that some of our activities have it, otherwise our lives have no meaning. Whether or not our lives have meaning is precisely the question that troubles Tolstoy. But this question, for him, cannot be separated from the question of whether his activities have objective value – and, indeed, whether anything has. To simply be told that they must have this value if his life is to count as meaningful does nothing to assuage these anxieties.

🐾

I think the most reasonable interpretation of the debate between subjectivist and hybrid theories of meaning in life is, then, this: both theories are deeply flawed. Neither has a chance of working. Not in their current incarnations, anyway. If this assessment is correct, we need to think a little harder, and maybe change the framework of assumptions in which our thinking operates. I think the language of philosophers has sold us a certain picture of the available alternatives, and this picture is incomplete. When words such as engagement, or attraction, or grip come to define a debate, this just demonstrates the constitutive insipidities of the profession. Meaning in life is deeper than engagement. It is deeper than attraction, deeper than grip. It is need. Meaning in life arises from need. And deeper than need, always deeper than need, is love.

Sisyphus, we imagined earlier in a variation on the myth, was made happy by an intervention of the gods, who altered him in such a way that he took great pleasure in rolling large rocks up steep hills. Following the gods' intervention, this was what Sisyphus enjoyed doing more than anything else in the world, and the gods had guaranteed him eternal fulfilment. This intervention, it seems, would make Sisyphus's afterlife much happier than it formerly was, but no more meaningful. In fact, if anything, it might be less meaningful. Any kind of dignity Sisyphus possessed – in his contempt for the gods and his refusal to be broken by them – would be lost in this intervention by them, leaving Sisyphus with the status of a deluded puppet.

There is a difference, vast and deep, between the happiness of this deluded Sisyphus, rolling his rock up a hill just so he can do so over and over again, and the happiness of Shadow, exiling his iguanas across the water just so he can return and do the same thing tomorrow and every day thereafter. The happiness of Sisyphus is a false happiness since it does not originate in who and what he truly is. It emanates from a version of Sisyphus twisted into something he is not. Shadow's happiness, I have argued, is different. His happiness is an expression of who and what he is. His engagement – his valuing of the chase – springs from his nature. Issuing from his nature, Shadow's happiness is, we might say, *authentic* happiness. Happiness that is genuinely his. Warped by the gods, Sisyphus's happiness is ineluctably inauthentic. It is not really his happiness because it does not issue from his nature. It is an aberration. It is no part of Sisyphus's nature to find happiness in rolling rocks. But it is part of Shadow's nature to find happiness in chasing iguanas. Shadow's happiness is, therefore, authentic, and it is this authentic happiness that supplies his life with meaning.

What, you might be wondering, is the difference between what the gods did to Sisyphus to make him happy and what we have done to Shadow, and to all our dogs to a greater or lesser extent? The gods intervened in the *life* – or, more accurately, the afterlife – of Sisyphus to change his character and allow him to find happiness in his punishment. We, on the other hand, intervene in the *histories* of dogs to change their character. There is a difference. The things that happen within a life are what we might call, borrowing from Aristotle, accidents. The gods decided to alter Sisyphus's character, but they might not have. Whether

Sisyphus finds satisfaction in rolling rocks up hills is a contingent matter, depending on an arbitrary decision of the gods. Things, in fact, turned out a certain way, but the gods might easily have made a different decision with different consequences.

Things that happen within a life are contingent. They might just as easily not have happened, or they might have happened differently. Once, however, they become part of your history – once they are fed into a story that began long before you were born – they move from the realm of contingency to that of necessity. They are now so thoroughly woven into the story that it can no longer be told without them. No longer accidents, these events are solidified by history, to be gradually transformed into the essence of those who undergo them.

This, I should emphasize, is just a description of the difference between events that happen in a life and events that happen in the history that feeds into a life and decisively shapes its general contours. Sometimes, the mere sight of a description tempts people to draw a moral conclusion. There is nothing moral to see here, not in anything I am saying, at any rate. Am I saying that it is a good thing that Shadow was selectively bred to have certain characteristics? No. I am describing what has happened, not advocating it. Obviously, selective breeding can have effects that can be morally assessed. The selective breeding that led to flat-nosed dogs with breathing difficulties is a moral travesty. The hip dysplasia that afflicts so many large dogs today is a morally reprehensible result of selective breeding. So too is the astonishing aggression of some breeds which, in combination with an inexperienced or feckless owner, can result in tragic consequences. These effects of history, and the decisions that led to them, can be morally assessed. But my claim is not a moral one. I am merely describing the difference between history and life, between essence and accident. Shadow's aggression is, in many ways, unfortunate, drastically narrowing the contours of his world, but on the other hand, history comes with certain advantages. History gives you a nature, and from nature can spring meaning in your life.

Meaning in life is authentic happiness. Meaning in life is always a joyful expression of one's nature. This, it is important to realize, is still a recognizably subjectivist account. Meaning in life still stems from one's valuing, rather than from any objective counterpart – but always valuing of a certain sort, a valuing that stems from one's nature; a valuing that issues from what one essentially is. This form of subjectivism can avoid the standard objections to subjectivist accounts of life's meaning – the sorts of objections that motivated the hybrid theory.

This new form of subjectivism does not make meaning in life ubiquitous. Meaning in life is not found wherever there is subjective engagement but only in specific instances of this engagement: instances that emanate from one's nature. Moreover, it is, in this account, possible to be mistaken about whether one's life has meaning. One can be mistaken about whether the joy one feels in an activity is an expression of one's nature – mistakenly thinking that it is not when it is, or that it is when it is not. Happy Sisyphus makes a mistake of this second sort – thinking that the joy he feels comes from him, from his nature, when it really comes from the gods. The ubiquity and infallibility objections, therefore, have no purchase against this form of subjectivism about life's meaning. Moreover, since the hybrid theory was introduced as a response to precisely these two objections, this renders the hybrid theory superfluous.

This version of a subjectivist account of life's meaning, therefore, has many advantages over the standard versions of subjectivism. Nevertheless, it shares with its standard counterparts one striking implication. The lives of dogs are, typically, more meaningful than those of humans; this conclusion is inescapable. When philosophers talk of subjective engagement, or of subjective attraction, or of being subjectively gripped by an activity, these are anaemic expressions, their apparent bloodlessness supposedly underwriting greater precision or utility. But this is an illusion. What we are really talking about when we use these words is always love: the love of life and action. If we are not talking about love, I really don't think we have anything useful to say about life's meaning.

The lives of dogs are more meaningful than those

of humans because there is more love in the lives of dogs. If you want to know what it is to love life, simply remember Hugo, with only moments of his life left to him, but magnificent still, his bite sleeve clamped tightly in his jaws, temporarily holding death at bay through the force of his love. Or if that is too sad – sometimes it is for me – think of Shadow, the young Shadow of my notes and drafts, thundering along the banks of a canal in Miami, scattering iguanas to the four corners of his small world.

Meaning in life is, ultimately, a subjective phenomenon best accommodated by a subjectivist theory. If this is correct, then, in the end, meaning in life comes down to love. The more love there is in a life, the more meaning this life thereby contains. The more you love your life, where this love is an expression of your nature, true and untainted, the more meaning there is in your life. To love what you do, when what you do is an expression of what you are, is at the same time to love yourself. Dogs love their lives more than we love ours. That is why their lives are more meaningful than ours.

As far as the meaning of life goes, dogs have notable advantages over us. Not being split down the middle by reflection, they have only one life to live. We live two lives, of dubious compatibility. There is the life that we live, but there is also the life that we scrutinize and evaluate. One can only expect that the single life of a dog would be more precious to it than either of our two lives are to us. We can never love each of our lives completely. After all, each life tears us out of the other. We can never love our two lives with the passion of a dog, near death, who held his bite sleeve firmly in his jaws. Nor with the passion of a dog who, in pursuit of iguanas, will run and run until his heart is ready to burst. A dog only has one life, and of it he is actor and not spectator, author and not critic. A dog loves his one life with everything he has because it is all he has. That is why there is more meaning in his life than there is in mine.

There is, however, more to it than a proliferation of lives. Meaning in life is authentic happiness, and happiness is authentic if it springs from nature. Dogs, however, have a nature in a much more robust sense than we do. The nature of a dog is heavy, a granite slab of essence. Our natures, however, have fractured beneath reflection's hard stare. To the extent that any of us have a nature at all, it is insubstantial, diaphanous, perhaps even gossamer thin. What we call our natures are, for us, merely an initial basis for further negotiation. We are self-interpreting creatures, and as such we have the most attenuated natures of all animals.

Shadow's nature, like that of any working-line German shepherd, is a little idiosyncratic in some respects. A working-line shepherd is, in part, a flock guardian. When the German shepherd breed was created by Max von Stephanitz, it was born of various lines of local working sheep dogs. However, when you look at many other flock guardian dogs – I have in mind the Caucasian Ovcharka, the central Asian shepherd, the Turkish Kangal and similar breeds – you will encounter a somewhat different profile and different resulting values. What you will typically find is high reactivity: aggression specifically directed towards other dogs and strangers. I have met some of these dogs. Many of them could give even Shadow a stern lesson in reactive aggression. Reactivity is, for obvious reasons, a desirable feature to have in a flock guardian. Dogs, wolves, rustlers – the flock may need to be protected from all of these. But what you don't find in these dogs is a high prey drive. Active aggression levels are generally low. The reasons for this are, again, obvious. A high prey drive in a dog entrusted to guard animals which, in other circumstances, might have been natural prey would not be a good idea.

What is quite unusual, if by no means unique, about the history of German shepherds is that they are flock guardians with a high prey drive. There are reasons for this. They are not just flock guardians, they are also herding dogs – which requires at least some minimal level of prey drive. And their employment has gradually spread out into other domains, such as the police and the military. For this, they needed to be highly trained. The best way of training a dog such as this is by utilizing its prey drive. A high-prey-drive dog wants to chase. And if you have something he can chase – a stick, a ball, a football remnant; in principle, most things will do – the dog will quickly become very cooperative, highly motivated to do what you would like him to do. A high prey drive, therefore, became a very desirable character trait for a German shepherd to have. And today, a shepherd that has it will command far more money than one that does not, precisely because it will be more trainable. Accordingly, working-line shepherds have been bred for prey drive too.

German shepherds are not unique in having an idiosyncratic history. The same is true of many herding dogs. For our purposes of understanding meaning in life, Shadow will more than suffice. In Shadow, because of his history, we find both traits. His nature, together with his behaviour on this canal, day in, day out for most of his life, has been an expression of this dual nature. What he is doing, every day, is a perfect expression of both his active and his reactive aggression. The former drives him to hunt. The latter drives him to guard. This is a human distinction, and I am sure Shadow would recognize no difference between the two. Hunting and guarding for him would just be different aspects of the same thing, two sides of a single coin. He is not hunting *and* guarding. He is hunting-guarding. If he had a word for what he did, he might, I suppose, call it *hurding*.

Hurding is the purest expression of Shadow's history, and thereby the purest expression of what his history has made him. In his pursuit of iguanas – his hurding – he finds joy that erupts from his nature; joy that captures and expresses this nature. This is why there is meaning in Shadow's life. This is how he answered the challenge of Sisyphus effortlessly, without even knowing there was a challenge to be answered.

My nature is far more attenuated. As far as my nature is concerned, there is not only what I am, there is also what I think about what I am. There is how I feel about it. There is how I interpret what I am, how I allot significance to the different events and circumstances that make me this way. Something happens to me, for good or ill, and I must now interpret the significance of this. What does it mean for me? How does it fit into my life? What are the consequences of this for me going forward? My nature is always a work in progress, a matter of my delicate and ongoing interpretative efforts. Meaning in life is happiness that erupts from nature. But there is little in my nature that is fixed. My nature is soft, pliable. It is, more than anything, labile: the attempts of others to interpret me might easily feed into my own interpretative efforts. There is no firm foundation in my nature to provide a springboard from which happiness might spring forth. That is why Shadow's life is more meaningful than mine.

᎗

Hugo loved his brothers, my sons, almost as much as he loved his bite sleeve. On the day of his death, we had told them a vet was coming to visit Hugo, but did not elaborate further. They were still young enough to assume that the vet was coming to make him better. Wanting to spare them, we had sent them upstairs to play while the vet did her work. The first injection was to render him unconscious rather than kill him. Sleep embraced him in seconds. In those few, fleeting, seconds of consciousness that remained in his life, Hugo managed to demonstrate what he had been all about. The pain dropped from his face, and his chin slowly sank to the ground, settling on the cool white tiles. At this very moment, there was a sound from upstairs. I don't remember what it was. Maybe laughter. Maybe they were arguing. I remember the incongruity, but I don't remember the noise precisely. As Hugo faded into darkness, he seemingly had one functioning body part remaining – his ear, specifically his left one. This ear shot bolt upright and pivoted in the direction of the sound. *Are they all right?* And then Hugo was gone. It was a heartbreakingly appropriate punctuation to a life that was defined by love. His life punctuated with his life's essence. That is a death few can dream of. My memory's grip on Hugo is slowly slipping. More and more I find it harder to picture him. Soon all that will be left to me will be an image of a single ear, pirouetting in the direction of love. I will count myself lucky to have that.

I haven't talked much about Brenin in this book, nor Nina or Tess. They have made the occasional appearance – as three canine salmon leaping above seas of barley, and as one recidivist cow-dung addict – but their appearances have been quite sparse and muted.

The Happiness of Dogs

There were some other books I have written to which they made more substantial contributions, and their absence in this one surprised me. Before I began writing this book, I had anticipated more. I shouldn't have.

Time takes everything in the end. It has taken the pain of Brenin's death, once raw and fathomless. It has also taken Brenin. Time's arrow heals everything in the end, but only by entropy, only by erasure. Time has taken Nina. It has taken Tess. What remain, in my conventional mind at least, are momentary, and fragmentary, impressions – vague suggestions, mutterings and murmurings, where memories used to be. My memories of them now can only be found in my extended mind. In books I have written. Books that I have written precisely so I may remember.

Where do our memories go when we lose them? My sons, once upon a time when they were very young, asked me this. It's a good question – I think you have to be very young to ask a really good question – and one that I spent quite some time, I'm talking about a decade or more, trying to answer. The answer, I think, is that, sometimes, they live on in a new form. What that is may vary. Sometimes they live on as behaviour, difficult to understand without full acquaintance with a person's history. Sometimes they live on as moods, that may last a lifetime or vanish as quickly as they came. But sometimes, just sometimes, they will live on as something else.

Some of my memories have a grim destiny. They will live on – re-emerge into the world – as ideas. For me, an idea is just a perfunctory summary of a memory I once had. An idea is just a memory drained of life; a memory that must be reanimated. The fact that I have chosen a life filled with ideas, I suspect, shows just how hard I must have tried to hold on to my memories. But permanence and unchangingness are not the way of memory, and as the poet Rainer Maria Rilke once noted, the most important thing with memories is to let them go and then have the immense patience to wait for them to return; when they do, they will come back in a new form, as glance and gesture, nameless, and no longer to be distinguished from who we are. Unable, in the end, to protect my memories by holding on to them, I defend them by letting them go, and then defending the ideas they eventually become. I try to protect with argument that which I could not protect with memory. That is the best I can do at reanimation.

In this sense, all the memories of my dogs are here in these pages, even the memories I no longer have. Brenin is here, and so too are Nina and Tess. Hugo is here. All these years later, his bite sleeve still rests in the garden. I have neither the heart nor the temerity to remove it. Shadow is here most of all, as a still-living, still-breathing book of memories. All these memories of those that have gone, and of those that will go, easily admit of perfunctory summary. This is the idea my memories have become: meaning in life is authentic happiness. Meaning in life exists wherever happiness erupts from nature. If you want to know the meaning of life, get a dog.

The Happiness of Dogs

Without uttering a word, my dogs tell me of a time before The Fall. Through them, I remember a time before reflection's canyon had opened within me, a time when I was one man and not two, when I had but one nature, one history and one life, a life that I loved with one heart and one mind, undivided. I will never walk in the Garden again. My exile is complete and irrevocable. Yet my dogs occasionally allow me to glimpse it, veiled, a distant shimmering on the far bank of the Jordan. As I walk with my dogs in memory, I find myself gazing sometimes towards Eden.

Further Reading

This book might have been subtitled, or even titled, if Granta had decided to go in a certain direction, *Barking and Nothingness*. There: I got that in before any clever reviewer has the chance. This is, in many ways, an existentialist tract. The influence of Albert Camus will be immediately obvious, from the opening chapter on. The great existential phenomenologist Jean-Paul Sartre will also be evident in many parts of this book. Personally, I think his greatness attaches to the phenomenologist in him rather than the existentialist. My first recommendation for further reading is pretty much anything that Camus wrote, or that Sartre wrote before – and I should emphasize this – his *Critique of Dialectical Reason*. I don't know what kind of trauma led him to write this later work. There is no need to concern yourself with it or with any of his subsequent philosophical works.

The work of John Gray – *Straw Dogs* and most of what he has written thereafter – has no doubt also insinuated itself into the thoughts contained in this book. The books before *Straw Dogs* were good too. Personally, I loved *Mill on Liberty*. But that's not the kind of thing I have in mind here. I disagree with John on many things, undoubtedly, but they are the sorts of disagreements you can only have with someone with whom you agree on so very much. So my second recommendation for further reading goes without saying. My other recommendations follow in a little more detail.

Chapter 1: Shadow's Rock

Anyone familiar with the work of Richard Taylor will see that my discussion of the Sisyphus myth has been heavily influenced by his work. See his *Good and Evil* (1970/1999, New York: Prometheus Books). Taylor did flip-flop once or twice about the implications of the myth for the question of meaning in life. There is no harm in that. It's hard! The 'happy Sisyphus' variation on the myth is his idea originally, as is the transformation of his rock into a pebble.

The classic existentialist treatment of the myth can be found in Albert Camus, *The Myth of Sisyphus and Other Essays* (1942, Paris: Gallimard; English translation by Justin O'Brien, 1955, New York: Alfred A. Knopf). The most accessible recent edition is the Penguin Classic version (with the same translator).

If you are interested in Schutzhund training for your dog, I recommend the classic work, Susan Barwig and

Further Reading

Stewart Hilliard's *Schutzhund: Theory and Training Methods* (1991, New York: Wiley). It's not for every dog. Hugo wasn't impressed. But if your dog is anything like Shadow, he or she will probably love it.

Chapter 2: The Unexamined Life

The story of Socrates' trial and death is told in Plato's *Apology*. It's a slim volume, and the most bang for your buck might be to buy it as part of the five-book (but still slim) volume, *Plato: Five Dialogues: Euthyphro, Apology, Crito, Meno, Phaedo*, ed. John Cooper, trans. G. M. A. Grube (2002, New York: Hackett).

Heidegger's notion of the *unheimlich* – the eerie, the unhomed – is found in his very large book, *Being and Time*. For English readers, there is a choice of translation. You have the 1962 John Macquarrie and Edward Robinson translation (Blackwell) or the more recent Joan Stambaugh translation (1996, Albany, NY: SUNY Press). Take your pick.

Alexander Luria and Lev Vygotsky's classic study of the consequences of the development of external forms of information storage – such as writing – can be found in translation in *Ape, Primitive Man and Child: Essays in the History of Behavior* (1992, Boca Raton, FL: CRC Press).

The Happiness of Dogs

Chapter 3: Mirror, Mirror

The classic study that became known as the mirror test is Gordon G. Gallup's 'Chimpanzees: self-recognition', *Science* (2 January 1970), 167, 86–7.

The distinction between reflective and pre-reflective self-awareness plays an important role in my book *Can Animals Be Persons?* (spoiler alert, yes, they can) (2019, New York: Oxford University Press). See especially chapters 6, 7 and 10.

Marc Bekoff's original version of the yellow snow test can be found in his 'Observations of scent marking and discriminating self from others by a domestic dog (*Canis familiaris*)', *Behavioural Processes* (15 August 2001), 55(2), 75–9.

For Alexandra Horowitz's inspired work with dog urine, see her 'Smelling themselves: dogs investigate their own odours longer when modified in an "olfactory mirror" test', *Behavioural Processes* (October 2017), 143, 17–24. For Roberto Gatti's work, on which she builds, see (2016) 'Self-consciousness: beyond the looking-glass and what dogs found there', *Ethology, Ecology & Evolution* (November 2015), 28(2), 232–40.

Sartre's distinction between reflective and pre-reflective self-awareness is a centrepiece of his *Being and Nothingness*. As with Heidegger's *Being and Time*, English speakers have a choice of two translations: the classic Hazel E. Barnes translation (Methuen), and the much more recent Sarah Richmond translation (Washington Square Press). Any quotations are from

Further Reading

the Barnes translation, but I've heard very good things about Richmond's alternative.

I mention this one only for the masochists among the readership: Kant's distinction between what he called 'empirical' and 'transcendental' forms of apperception – or what I am calling reflection and pre-reflection – is found in his monumental *Critique of Pure Reason*. I won't even go into editions and translations because, whichever one you choose, it's largely incomprehensible. Good luck!

For an excellent overview and analysis of predictive processing, two books by Andy Clark are exemplary. There is his *Surfing Uncertainty: Prediction, Action, and the Embodied Mind* (2016, New York: Oxford University Press) and his *The Experience Machine: How Our Minds Predict and Shape Reality* (2023, London: Allen Lane).

Edmund Husserl, in effect, began the predictive approach to seeing. See his *Ideas Pertaining to a Pure Phenomenology and to a Phenomenological Philosophy*, trans. T. Klein and W. Pohl (1980, The Hague: Martinus Nijhoff). For an excellent recent account inspired, if somewhat loosely, by Husserl's account, see Alva Noë's *Action in Perception* (2006, Cambridge, MA: MIT Press).

The classic study by Brian Hare, Josep Call and Michael Tomasello on perspective taking in chimpanzees is their paper 'Do chimpanzees know what conspecifics know?', in *Animal Behaviour* (January 2001), 61(1), 139–51.

The Happiness of Dogs

Chapter 4: A Gambler's Freedom

Sartre's account of freedom and resulting anguish (and his example of the titular gambler) is in *Being and Nothingness*, Part 1. Spinoza's account of freedom is developed most fully in his *Ethics*. Probably the most easily accessible version is the 1996 Penguin Classics edition, translated by Edwin Curley.

Chapter 5: Good Dogs

My more academic musings on the possibility of morality in animals can be found in my book *Can Animals Be Moral?* (2012, New York: Oxford University Press). Also well worth a read is Marc Bekoff and Jessica Pierce's book, *Wild Justice* (2009, Chicago: University of Chicago Press).

Darwin's thoughts on the possibility of moral behaviour in animals can be found in his *Descent of Man* (1871), chapter 3 or 4 (depending on the edition). Frans de Waal has also written extensively about this topic, from within a Darwinian framework. See especially his *Primates and Philosophers* (2006, Princeton, NJ: Princeton University Press) and *The Age of Empathy* (2009, New York: Crown).

Belinda Recio's lovely book, marred only by a foreword she inadvisably asked me to write, is *When Animals Rescue: Amazing True Stories about Heroic and Helpful Creatures* (2021, New York: Skyhorse Publishing).

Further Reading

For Aristotle's reflective view of moral virtue, *The Nicomachean Ethics* is best – with a number of translations and publishers from which to choose. For Kant's similarly reflective view of moral action, see his *Critique of Practical Reason*. A very good recent defence of the Kantian picture – with which I therefore disagree vehemently – can be found in Christine Korsgaard's book, *Fellow Creatures: Our Obligations to the Other Animals* (2018, Oxford: Oxford University Press).

For the idea of anthropofabulation, see Cameron Buckner's 'Morgan's canon, meet Hume's dictum: avoiding anthropofabulation in cross-species comparisons', *Biology & Philosophy* (2013), 28(5), 853–71.

Chapter 6: A Design for Life

See Alfred North Whitehead, *An Introduction to Mathematics* (1911, London: Williams & Norgate) for his views on automaticity.

One of my favourite studies ever because it does such a great job of isolating the canine aptitude for, and contempt of, thinking is Á. Erdöhegyi, J. Topál, Z. Virányi & Á. Miklósi, 'Dog-logic: inferential reasoning in a two-way choice task and its restricted use', *Animal Behaviour* (October 2007), 74(4), 725–37.

For a lucid account of the domestication of the dog, with the co-domestication of humans thrown in for good measure, you could take a look at Laura Hobgood-Oster, *A Dog's History of the World: Canines and the*

Domestication of Humans (2014, Waco, TX: Baylor University Press).

The classic thought experiment involving the imaginary Otto is to be found in Andy Clark and Dave Chalmers, 'The extended mind', *Analysis* (January 1998), 58(1), 7–19. Clark, however, had been writing about this idea long before then. See his *Being There: Putting Brain, Body, and World Together Again* (1998, Cambridge, MA: MIT Press) for a summary of a decade or so of work on this topic. My contributions include *The Body in Mind: Understanding Cognitive Processes* (1999, Cambridge: Cambridge University Press) and, my favourite, *The New Science of the Mind: From Extended Mind to Embodied Phenomenology* (2010, Cambridge, MA: MIT Press).

John Rawls's advocacy of a rational plan for life can be found in his *A Theory of Justice* (1971, Cambridge, MA: Harvard University Press). For a useful discussion of the idea of a rational plan for life and the distinction between a plan and a voyage, see David Heyd and Franklin G. Miller, 'Life plans: do they give meaning to our lives?' *The Monist* (1 January 2010), 93(1), 17–37.

Chapter 7: Just Dogs with the Yips

Ludwig Wittgenstein, *Tractatus Logico-Philosophicus* (originally published in 1921 and translated into English the following year by C. K. Ogden). A strange

Further Reading

but brilliant book, representing a systematic approach to philosophy that Wittgenstein later abandoned.

The distinction between the body-as-object and the body-as-lived (Husserl referred to them as *Körper* and *Leib*, respectively) is a staple of the phenomenological tradition in philosophy. The idea of the body-as-lived as revealing activity is suggested by some typically cryptic remarks of Sartre in *Being and Nothingness*. Once again, I have tried to put some flesh on the bones of this Sartrean intuition. Sartre's discussion of shame can also be found in *Being and Nothingness*, Part 3.

The idea of absurdity as a clash between two perspectives we can take on life, both of which can't be true but neither of which we can abandon, is a theme of some important work by Thomas Nagel. See especially his paper 'The absurd', which can be found in an edited collection of his work, *Mortal Questions* (1979, New York: Cambridge University Press).

Moritz Schlick's claim that the meaning of life is play can be found in his 1927 paper, 'On the meaning of life', published in his *Philosophical Papers: Vol. II* (1979, Dordrecht: D. Reidel). It is reprinted in E. D. Klemke and Steven M. Cahn (eds), *The Meaning of Life: A Reader*, 3rd ed. (2008, New York: Oxford University Press), pp. 62–71.

For the distinction between choking and the yips, I am grateful to David Papineau. See his *Knowing the Score* (2017, London: Constable).

The Happiness of Dogs

Chapter 8: Sometimes Toward Eden

Susan Wolf's account of meaning in life is developed most fully in her book, *Meaning in Life and Why It Matters* (2010, Princeton. NJ: Princeton University Press).

The Tolstoy quote is from his *A Confession: The Gospel in Brief. What I Believe*, trans. Aylmer Maude (1921, London: Oxford University Press), pp. 16–17.

My ruminations on the subject of memory, including the idea of what I called Rilkean memory, can be found in my *Memory and the Self* (2016, New York: Oxford University Press). Rilke's suggestive remarks are found in his only excursion into the art form of the novel (he was primarily a poet), originally published in 1910, *The Notebooks of Malte Laurids Brigge*, trans. E. Snow (2022, New York: W. W. Norton).

The expression 'a glacial expanse, dark and nameless' echoes the last line of the poem 'Old Man' by Edward Thomas.

Acknowledgements

My thanks to everyone at Granta for helping bring this book into the world. Very special thanks to my editor, Bella Lacey, for her patient and immensely helpful comments on earlier drafts of this book. My thanks to Mandy Woods for outstanding copy-editing. It is great to be working with Christine Lo again. Thanks, finally, to Isabella Depiazzi for helping to ensure this book reaches as wide an audience as possible.

If the central contention of this book is correct, it seems I owe a debt, of a broadly pedagogical sort, to a number of dogs. So, thank you, Boots, Sandy, Pharaoh, Brenin, Nina, Tess, Hugo and Shadow. Not all of you made it into these pages, but I remember you all with love and gratitude.

Finally, thanks to my family, to my wife and my sons. This book, as always, is dedicated to them.

Index

aboriginal cultures, 47
absurdity, 187
Adam and Eve, 43–4, 48–9, 51, 192
affection, 139–41
affordances, 67
aggression, active and reactive, 19–20, 23–4, 27–8, 224–5
akrasia, 126
Ali, Muhammad, 198
allergies, 21
alligators, 163
Alzheimer's disease, 157
American bulldogs, 7
Amphipolis, battle of, 35
anguish, 103
anthropofabulation, 121
Aristotle, 117, 119–20, 125–6, 133, 144, 151, 165, 218
Armour, Tommy, 191
art forms, 50
Athens, ancient, 5, 33–5
athletic endeavours, 50
Attila the Hun, 212
autism, 136

baboons, 115
bad faith, 108–9
bears, 126
Bekoff, Marc, 60, 139
Belgian Malinois, 18
beliefs, 40, 75, 81–3, 102, 126, 157–8, 186
Belyaev, Dmitri, 156
Berkeley, Busby, 9
Bible, 44
body-as-lived and body-as-object, 180–3, 194–5
bonobos, 55, 78
brains, 45–6, 68–9, 80, 162
    anterior cingulate cortex, 138
    anterior insular cortex, 138
    and left gaze bias, 154
    somatosensory cortex, 138
    visual cortex, 68
Brenin, 26, 56–8, 67–9, 87, 98–100, 199, 227–9
Buckner, Cameron, 121
Bulger, Jamie, 128

Call, Josep, 74
Camus, Albert, 3–4, 16, 28, 202–3
Capone, Al, 21
Cartesian space, 70
Caucasian Ovcharkas, 224
central Asian shepherds, 224
Chalmers, David, 157–8, 161
character and destiny, 16, 27
chimpanzees, 55, 74–5, 78, 162
choices, 51, 102, 105–7
choking, 191
chordates, 45
Chrysippus, 149–50
Clark, Andy, 157–8, 161
commitment, 4–6, 31–2, 81–5, 87, 116, 124, 177, 190, 196
Conan the Barbarian, 19
consciousness, 4–5, 48, 52, 54–5, 88, 90–5, 103, 105, 180–1, 193, 227
    and intentionality, 91–2, 94, 100–1
constructivism, 209–10
contingency–consequence pairings, 69, 82
Craig, William Lane, 200–1
Csikszentmihalyi, Mihaly, 50

Darwin, Charles, 110, 115–16, 144, 156
de Waal, Frans, 116, 144
death, 179

Index

Delium, battle of, 35
Descartes, René, 5, 84, 151, 165
dichotomies, 77, 79
disjunctive syllogisms, 150, 152, 154, 157, 160, 162
distress, 134–7, 143
   intentional object, 136
Doberman Pinschers, 112
dogs
   aggression, 17–20, 224–5
   barking, 160
   and causal reasoning, 162–4
   domestication, 155–7, 160, 162
   and empathy, 136–7
   and extended mind, 157, 164–5
   and freedom, 86–90, 102, 104, 109
   hip dysplasia, 219–20
   and logical reasoning, 149–50, 152–3
   and meaningful life, 28–9, 221–3
   and meta-cognition, 75
   and moral behaviour, 113–15, 119, 125–6, 139, 143
   pictures of, 98–100
   reading human faces, 154–5
   selective breeding, 219–20
   and self-awareness, 55–6, 59–60, 71–2
   spontaneity, 169–70
   training, 19–25, 140–2
   urine, 60–4
dolphins, 55, 79
domestication, syndrome, 156
ducks, 23–4, 27, 67, 134, 173
Dutch herding dogs, 18
Dutch shepherds, 18

egrets, 19, 27
elephants, 55, 79, 186
emotions, 120, 133, 142, 144–6, 154, 157
   emotional contagion, 134–7
empathy, 134–7, 139, 143, 146
enjoyment, 203
Enlightenment, 5
evolution, 44, 46–7, 138, 156
existential phenomenology, 47
extended minds, 157–8, 161, 164, 228
external information-bearing structures, 46, 159–61, 165
eye contact, 55
eyes, 46

Fall, the, 44, 48, 50, 86, 199, 230
family-values, 34

fears, 40, 42, 65, 73, 75, 83, 102, 180, 183
flow, 50–1
footballs, 147–9, 224
Frank, Harry, 163
free will, 188
freedom, 86–90, 102–4, 109
Freud, Sigmund, 79

Gallup, Gordon, 53, 55
Garden of Eden, 14, 44, 51, 86, 170, 199, 230
Gatti, Roberto, 62
geese, 27, 30–1, 41, 134
German shepherds, 1–2, 8, 18–19, 24, 26, 56, 171, 223–5
God, 200–2
Gogol, Nikolai, 215
Golden Rule, 118
golf, 191–2
gorillas, 55
Graf, Steffi, 191
great apes, 74, 152
groundlessness, 105–9, 131

Haifa vom Schotterhof, 17
happiness, authentic, 5, 28, 218, 220, 223, 229
Hare, Brian, 74
Heidegger, Martin, 49, 67, 93
Heraclitus of Ephesus, 16, 27
herons, 27
hopes, 40–2, 54, 65, 73, 75, 83, 102, 180, 183
Horowitz, Alexandra, 62–3
Hugo, 26, 171–8, 185, 190, 196, 222, 226–7
humanism, 200
Hume, David, 133, 139
Hurricane Irma, 31
Husserl, Edmund, 67, 90–1
hybrid theory, 204–5, 208–11, 213–16, 220–1

ibises, 19, 27
iguanas, 8–9, 12–14, 19–20, 23, 27–8, 66–7, 69–71, 81–2, 87, 89, 134, 147, 155, 173, 197, 217–18, 222–3, 225
impartiality, 124
Inchydoney Island, 98, 100
inhibition, 139, 141–4, 146
intelligence, 79, 162, 164

243

intentionality, 91–2, 94, 97–8, 100–1, 130
invasive species, 13
involution, 47

James, William, 17
Jethro, 60, 139, 143
Julius Caesar, 212

Kant, Immanuel, 54, 64, 117–18, 120, 125–7, 129–33, 144
  ought implies can, 125–6
Khan, 112–13, 115, 123
Koehler method, 142
kvinus, 159

left gaze bias, 154
Lilica, 114–15
Liszt, Franz, 50
lives
  examined life, 34–5, 37, 39, 43–4, 167
  life-as-lived and life-as-object, 183–8
  meaningful life, 12, 15, 28–9, 37, 186, 199–208, 212–17, 220–3, 226
  two lives, 178, 180, 182, 185, 199, 222–3
  unexamined life, 30–3, 35–6, 38–9, 43
literacy, 47, 159, 161, 164
Llinás, Rodolfo, 45
Luria, Alexander, 47, 159, 161

malamutes, 26, 56, 99, 163
manatees, 28
Manchester United FC, 178, 191
manta rays, 55, 79
Marlowe, Christopher, 201
meaningless activities, 213–15
measles, 189
memory, biological, 47, 80
memory loss, 157
mental acts, 40–3, 54, 91–2, 94–5, 100, 180, 182
Merleau-Ponty, Maurice, 67
Milton, John, 197
mirror neurons, 138
mirror test, 53–5, 59–60, 64–5, 72–3, 76, 78, 80, 180
Molière, 216
monkeys, 152

moral behaviour, 113–33, 139, 142–6
  ought implies can (Kant), 125–6
  one-thought-too-many failures (Williams), 123–4
  proto morality, 116
moral value, 211–12
motivations, 20, 59–60, 115–26, 129–33, 143–5
mountain climbing, 214
Museum of Modern Art, 157–8, 161

Nagel, Thomas, 187
neoteny, 156
New Caledonian crows, 162
Newfoundland dogs, 115
Nina, 26, 56–8, 67, 87, 98–100, 110–12, 115, 119–20, 135, 227–9
Novotná, Jana, 191

objectivism, 204, 208, 210, 212, 214–16
octopuses, 162
Oracle of Delphi, 33
orangutans, 55, 78
'oughts', logical and epistemic, 126–7

parvovirus, 189
Peloponnesian War, 35
pictures and photographs, 98–100
pigeons, 55, 79
Plato, 30, 32–3, 44, 151, 153, 165
play, 78, 190–1, 196
poisoning, 13–14
Potidaea, battle of, 35
predictive processing, 67–9
pre-literate cultures, 159, 161, 164
pre-reflection, 65–6, 70–2, 76–8, 181–2, 193
probabilities, 31
proofing, 22–3
Proust, Marcel, 79
Pushkin, Alexander, 216

Rathmore peninsula, 57
rational planning, 166–9
rationality, 4, 78, 133, 151, 166
rats, 58, 86–7
ravens, 152
reasoning, logical and causal, 149–50, 152–3, 162–4
Recio, Belinda, 112
reductio ad absurdum, 38

Index

reflection, 40–4, 48–51, 53–4, 56, 60–1, 64–6, 72–3, 76–90, 102, 109, 222–3, 230
 and body-as-object, 180, 187
 and commitment, 81–5
 and meta-cognition, 73, 75–7
 and moral behaviour, 115–17, 122–3, 130, 133, 144, 146
 and the yips, 191–2, 195–6
 see also pre-reflection
religious practices, 214
Rilke, Rainer Maria, 79, 229
Roman Empire, 212
Russell, Bertrand, 154

Saint-Germain royal gardens, 151
Sartre, Jean-Paul, 53–4, 64, 67, 71, 83, 86, 90–9, 101–5, 108, 130–1, 192–4
Schlick, Moritz, 190
Schutzhunde (protection dogs), 17–18, 20, 24
sea squirts, 45, 80
self-awareness, 40, 64–6, 71–3, 76–7, 82, 84
 and dogs, 55–6, 59–60, 71–2
 positional or reflective, 54
 three forms of, 76
 and vision, 71–2
self-examination, 31–3, 35–9, 43
self-reference, 54
sentences, 96–7
sentimentalism, 133, 139
Shadow, 1–8, 12–32, 40–1, 66–72, 81–5, 87, 89, 134, 139–43, 147–9, 165, 169–71, 173, 197, 199–200, 217–20, 222–6, 229
 aggression, 17–18, 26–8, 220, 225
 East German lineage, 8, 18, 24, 173
 training, 19–25
Shakespeare, William, 216
shame, 43–4, 184, 192, 194
shared representation systems, 137
sharpeagles, 17
silver foxes, 156
Sisyphus, 9–12, 14–16, 28–9, 199, 202, 214, 217–19, 221, 226
Smith, Adam, 139
snakes, 28, 113, 123
Socrates, 1, 5, 32–9, 43–4, 84, 167, 189
Sparta, 35
spines, 46

Spinoza, Baruch, 88–90, 102, 104, 109
squirrels, 67, 173
Stephanitz, Max von, 223
stimulus equivalence, 61–4
sub specie aeternitatis, 184
subjectivism, 177, 203–6, 209–11, 216, 220–2
supererogatory behaviour, 113–14

Tess, 26, 56–9, 87, 110–12, 115, 119–20, 135, 227–9
 dung-rolling behaviour, 58–9, 61–2, 67, 227
Thebes, 35
theory of mind, 73, 75
Thomas, Dylan, 6
Thompson, Robert, 128–9
Tolstoy, Leo, 215–16
Tomasello, Michael, 74
tool use, 78, 162
trainspotting, 205–7
transcendental apperception, 64
trespass, 20–1
Turkish Kangals, 224
turtles, 28

unheimlich (the term), 49
University of Miami, 17, 21–2, 24
utilitarianism, 118, 124

Venables, Jon, 128–9
vision, 179–80
 as predictive processing, 67–9
 and self-awareness, 71–2
vultures, 19–20, 27
Vygotsky, Lev, 47, 159, 161

Whitehead, Alfred North, 147, 153–5
Williams, Bernard, 123–4
Wittgenstein, Ludwig, 96, 171, 179
wolamutes, 173
Wolf, Susan, 204, 213, 215–16
wolfdogs, 26, 56, 99
wolves, 56, 99, 155–6, 163–4, 224
wrasse, 55–6, 79
writing, 46–7, 80, 162
Wundt, Wilhelm, 79

yellow snow test, 60–1, 64
yips, 191–2, 195–6

Zahn-Waxler, Carolyn, 136

About the Author

Mark Rowlands was born in Newport, Wales. He is a Professor of Philosophy at the University of Miami and the author of more than twenty books, including the bestselling *The Philosopher and the Wolf*, also published by Granta. His books have been translated into more than twenty languages.